Grammar, Usage, and Mechanics Book

McDougal Littell

GRADE SEVEN

Teaching

More Practice

Application

McDougal Littell
A HOUGHTON MIFFLIN COMPANY
Evanston, Illinois Boston Dallas

ISBN-13: 978-0-618-15376-3 ISBN-10: 0-618-15376-4

23 24 25 26 0868 15 14 13 12
4500369872

Contents

Special Features

The *Grammar, Usage, and Mechanics Copymasters/Workbook* contains a wealth of skill-building exercises.

Each lesson has different levels of worksheets. **Teaching** introduces the skill; **More Practice** and **Application** extend the skill with advanced exercises.

Each page focuses on one topic or skill. A brief instructional summary on the **Teaching** page is followed by reinforcement activities.

Key words and phrases are highlighted for greater clarity and ease of use.

When appropriate, example sentences demonstrate how to complete exercises.

Tabs make it easy to navigate the book.

Name ______________________________ Date ____________

Complete Subjects and Predicates

Teaching

A sentence is a group of words that expresses a complete thought. Every complete sentence has two basic parts: a subject and a predicate.

The **complete subject** includes all the words that tell whom or what the sentence is about.

Wildlife conservationists monitor endangered animals.

The **complete predicate** includes the verb and all the words that tell what the subject is or what the subject does.

Endangered animals need protection.

CHAPTER 1

Identifying Complete Subjects and Complete Predicates

Underline the complete subject once and the complete predicate twice.

EXAMPLE The blue whale needs protection from commercial hunters.

1. The clearing of forests destroys many animals' habitats.
2. Some animals cannot adapt to new environments.
3. New laws protect the habitat of many threatened animals.
4. American bison became an endangered species in the 1800s.
5. The bison herd is growing once again.
6. Dangerous chemicals in the water and on land poison some types of animals and birds.
7. National parks provide a safe place for animals to live.
8. The California condor population is getting bigger.
9. Many scientists are working to save the giant panda.
10. The Asiatic lion and the Bengal tiger still face extinction.
11. Endangered animals are the group most in danger of becoming extinct.
12. Threatened animals may be at risk as well.
13. Zoos raise some endangered animals in captivity.
14. Peregrine falcons and Hawaiian geese have been raised successfully this way.
15. Grown animals are released into wildlife refuges or national parks.
16. Pelican Island in Florida was the first federal wildlife refuge in the U. S.
17. The Fish and Wildlife Service helps to preserve endangered animals.
18. The World Wildlife Fund raises money for conservation programs.
19. About 40 kinds of birds became extinct in the last 200 years.
20. Two lost species are the passenger pigeon and the Carolina parakeet.
21. The California grizzly bear could not be saved from extinction.

Name ______________________ Date ______________

Complete Subjects and Predicates

Teaching

A sentence is a group of words that expresses a complete thought. Every complete sentence has two basic parts: a subject and a predicate.

The **complete subject** includes all the words that tell whom or what the sentence is about.

Wildlife conservationists monitor endangered animals.

The **complete predicate** includes the verb and all the words that tell what the subject is or what the subject does.

Endangered animals need protection.

CHAPTER 1

Identifying Complete Subjects and Complete Predicates

Underline the complete subject once and the complete predicate twice.

EXAMPLE The blue whale needs protection from commercial hunters.

1. The clearing of forests destroys many animals' habitats.
2. Some animals cannot adapt to new environments.
3. New laws protect the habitat of many threatened animals.
4. American bison became an endangered species in the 1800s.
5. The bison herd is growing once again.
6. Dangerous chemicals in the water and on land poison some types of animals and birds.
7. National parks provide a safe place for animals to live.
8. The California condor population is getting bigger.
9. Many scientists are working to save the giant panda.
10. The Asiatic lion and the Bengal tiger still face extinction.
11. Endangered animals are the group most in danger of becoming extinct.
12. Threatened animals may be at risk as well.
13. Zoos raise some endangered animals in captivity.
14. Peregrine falcons and Hawaiian geese have been raised successfully this way.
15. Grown animals are released into wildlife refuges or national parks.
16. Pelican Island in Florida was the first federal wildlife refuge in the U. S.
17. The Fish and Wildlife Service helps to preserve endangered animals.
18. The World Wildlife Fund raises money for conservation programs.
19. About 40 kinds of birds became extinct in the last 200 years.
20. Two lost species are the passenger pigeon and the Carolina parakeet.
21. The California grizzly bear could not be saved from extinction.

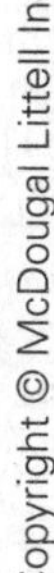

Name ______________________________ Date ______________

Complete Subjects and Predicates

More Practice

A. Identifying Complete Subjects and Predicates

Draw a vertical line between the complete subject and the complete predicate in each of the following sentences.

EXAMPLE Several animals | are endangered today.

1. Tropical forests contain more kinds of animals than any other place.
2. Biologists discovered 43 different ants in one tree in South America.
3. A change in the tropical forest affects many species.
4. Many conservationists are worried about the destruction of tropical forests.
5. Pollution harms some types of animals as well.
6. Acid rain kills some animals and fish.
7. State and federal authorities want lower pollution levels.
8. Overhunting in an area changes the animal population.
9. Species often cannot maintain themselves in the face of these problems.
10. Yellowstone National Park is one of the biggest wildlife refuges in the United States.

B. Using Complete Subjects and Predicates

On the line to the right of each item, write how each group of words could be used: **CS** for a complete subject or **CP** for a complete predicate. Then use each group of words in a complete sentence, adding a complete subject or complete predicate as needed.

EXAMPLE a beautiful bird *CS*
A beautiful bird landed on my windowsill.

1. a delicious picnic lunch ______________

____

2. marched down the street ______________

____

3. big cities ______________

____

4. won the race ______________

____

CHAPTER 1

Name ______________________________ Date ______________

Lesson 1 Complete Subjects and Predicates

Application

A. Revising by Adding Details

Add details to the subjects and predicates to make these simple sentences more interesting.

1. Fish swim.

____

2. Birds fly.

____

3. Lions roam.

____

4. Scientists study.

____

5. Turtles live.

____

6. Elephants travel.

____

CHAPTER 1

B. Writing with Complete Subjects and Complete Predicates

One student wrote these notes for a report. Because he was in a hurry, he wrote them as sentence fragments, not complete sentences. Review his notes, and rewrite the fragments as complete sentences with complete subjects and predicates. If you like, you may combine two or more fragments in a single sentence.

Successful conservation effort by Museum of Natural History. Eagle eggs found. Nest destroyed. Eggs in incubator at museum. Tried to get newly hatched eaglets to eat. Food from an eyedropper. Later, eagle's head hand puppet used to feed bits of meat. Museum built nest in tree. Taught birds to fly down from nest. Finally able to fly and get own food. Released into wildlife preserve with other eagles.

____

____

____

____

____

____

____

Name ________________________________ Date ______________

Simple Subjects

Teaching

The simple subject is the main word or words in the complete subject. Words that describe the subject are not part of the simple subject. In the following sentence, the simple subject is underlined.

People in a large city lead busy lives.

If a proper name is used as the subject, all parts of the name make up the simple subject.

Councilman Johnson in our ward cares about neighborhood concerns.

CHAPTER 1

Identifying Simple Subjects

Underline the simple subject in each sentence.

1. Life in the city is often hectic.
2. Ms. Hale took a cab to the convention center.
3. The airport closed because of the storm.
4. Many unhappy passengers were left stranded.
5. Shuttle buses took passengers to the hotel.
6. A large truck blocked the street in front of the apartment building.
7. Main Street in the downtown area was under construction.
8. Football fans gathered for the first game in the new stadium.
9. Mayor Thomas attended the game as a special guest.
10. The express train to New York left at six o'clock.
11. Students from the university volunteered as reading tutors at the nearby school.
12. Our civic orchestra gave a free concert at Public Square.
13. The art museum has a new exhibit on Egyptian art.
14. Two new office buildings just opened yesterday.
15. The library in my neighborhood hosted a speech by a famous author.
16. Rush-hour traffic was slowed by the heavy rains.
17. An emergency medical helicopter landed at the hospital.
18. Samantha stopped at the mall to look for some shoes.
19. A slow-moving street cleaner backed up traffic on the freeway for miles.
20. Wu moved into an apartment near school.
21. The freighter from Greece slowly approached the pier.
22. People on the docks prepared for its arrival.
23. Cities, with all their activities, are never boring.

Name ______________________________ Date ______________

Lesson 2

Simple Subjects

More Practice

A. Identifying Simple Subjects

Underline the simple subject in each of the following sentences.

1. Judge Lane presided over municipal court.
2. The airport terminal was crowded with holiday travelers.
3. Buses to downtown had standing room only.
4. Some people on their way to downtown hotels hailed cabs.
5. A free rock concert was held in the city park.
6. Captain Gomez of the police department directed the traffic unit during the president's visit.
7. The subways were nearly empty during the late night hours.
8. Trucks at the airport dropped off the packages for morning delivery to the coast.
9. The restaurant at the train station served only sandwiches and soups.
10. The firefighters welcomed visitors to an open house at the station.

B. Writing Simple Subjects

Choose one of the following words to complete each sentence below. Write the simple subject on the line.

buses	skyscraper	workers	museum	restaurants
trucks	traffic	stores	stoplight	sounds

1. The ______________ in the downtown area had big sales on nearly everything.
2. ______________ in the high-rise buildings saw the parade through their office windows.
3. Many ______________ from all over the city take riders to work every day.
4. A broken ______________ caused a traffic jam on Fifth Street.
5. The new ______________ under construction will have 50 floors plus a restaurant on the roof.
6. A ______________ highlighting the city's history will open soon.
7. ______________ around the stadium was moving smoothly with no problems.
8. Many neighborhood ______________ offer specials on ethnic foods.
9. ______________ filled with debris rumbled through the city on their way to the dump.
10. Loud cheering ______________ were coming from the baseball stadium.

Name ____________________ Date ____________

Lesson 2

Simple Subjects

Application

A. Writing Simple Subjects in Sentences

Use each of these words as the simple subject in a sentence.

1. traffic ____________________

____

2. buildings ____________________

____

3. streets ____________________

____

4. people ____________________

____

5. excitement ____________________

____

B. Revising

Read this paragraph carefully. In some sentences, the writer has left out the simple subjects. When you find a sentence without a simple subject, insert this proofreading symbol ^ and write a simple subject in the space above it.

EXAMPLE Some ^*cities* attract many visitors.

Visitors to a big city have many things to do and see. If you have the energy, the city has the activities. For example, the may have historical buildings for you to visit. If your tastes run to the artistic, try the art museum with its impressive collection of paintings and sculptures from around the world. A public filled with thousands of books and magazines is another excellent place to visit. A tourist may shop at many different stores. Offer the hungry visitor a variety of delicious meals. Fancy have plays or concerts nightly. A huge new for football or baseball games offers another type of entertainment. Most are not bored when they visit a city.

Name ______________________ Date ____________

Simple Predicates, or Verbs

Teaching

CHAPTER 1

The **simple predicate,** or **verb** is the main word or words in the complete predicate. In the following sentence, the simple predicate, or verb, is underlined.

> Many people <u>have</u> interesting hobbies.
> VERB (*have interesting hobbies* is the complete predicate)

The verb can be a single word as in the sentence above, or a verb phrase, as in the sentence below.

> Hobbies <u>can entertain</u> you for years.
> VERB PHRASE (*can entertain you for years* is the complete predicate)

Verbs are words used to express actions, conditions, or states of being. **Linking verbs** tell what the subject is. **Action verbs** tell what the subject does, even when the action cannot be seen.

Identifying Simple Predicates, or Verbs

Underline the simple predicate, or verb, in each sentence.

1. One popular hobby is stamp collecting.
2. Some people collect stamps from one country only.
3. Others save stamps from around the world.
4. Stamp collectors like rare or unusual stamps.
5. Books and magazines give valuable information about this hobby.
6. Some groups exchange special cards as their hobby.
7. Sports fans trade baseball, football, or basketball cards.
8. Different kinds of cards are everywhere.
9. Many people enjoy their coin collections.
10. Music provides a hobby for some.
11. People of all ages sing by themselves or in a choir.
12. Others play musical instruments for fun.
13. Still others listen to tapes and CDs.
14. More active people participate in sports.
15. Bowling is a relaxing hobby.
16. Hobbies include board games and card games.
17. Crafts attract hobbyists who are skillful with their hands.
18. Attractive pottery items start with a lump of clay.
19. Hand-sewn designs last for many years.
20. Model railroaders build whole landscapes for their trains.

Name ______________________ Date ____________

Simple Predicates, or Verbs

More Practice

A. Identifying Simple Predicates, or Verbs

Underline the simple predicate, or verb, in each of the following sentences.

1. Hobbies fill many leisure hours.
2. Your favorite hobby depends on your interests and skills.
3. Some hobbies develop into a lifetime activity.
4. People collect antiques, dolls, or autographs.
5. Others work with their hands.
6. Woodworking requires careful planning.
7. Models of airplanes or cars take many hours to assemble.
8. Quilters sew tiny pieces of cloth in a special design.
9. Photographers need special equipment for their hobby.
10. Painting is an interesting form of relaxation.

B. Writing Simple Predicates, or Verbs

Choose one of the following words to complete each sentence below. Write the simple predicate, or verb, on the line. After you use a word, cross it out.

build	collect	glue	buy	research
listen	cut	follow	thread	write

1. Crafters ______________ instructions step by step as they work.
2. Some people ______________ poetry as a hobby.
3. Jewelry makers ______________ bags of colored beads at the craft store.
4. Collage makers ______________ images on a surface with a special paste.
5. Music lovers ______________ to their favorite songs over and over.
6. Some crafters use sharp scissors to ______________ designs and patterns out of cloth and paper.
7. Sometimes rock hounds ______________ unusual stones to polish.
8. Railroad enthusiasts buy or ______________ bridges and other structures for their trains.
9. Weavers ______________ their looms with yarn or other material.
10. Antique collectors ______________ an item to determine its value.

Name ________________________________ Date ____________

Lesson 3

Simple Predicates, or Verbs

Application

A. Writing Simple Predicates, or Verbs, in Sentences

Use each of these words as the simple predicate, or verb, in a sentence.

1. collect ________________________________

2. sew ________________________________

3. buy ________________________________

4. build ________________________________

5. draw ________________________________

B. Revising

Read this paragraph carefully. In some sentences, the writer has left out the simple predicates, or verbs. When you find a sentence without a simple predicate, or verb, insert this proofreading symbol ^ and write a verb in the space above it.

EXAMPLE Making pottery ^*is* an interesting hobby.

Some hobbyists specialize in pottery making. A lump of clay becomes a work of art in their hands. First, they the color and type of clay. Then they decide how to make their object. For the coil method, they the clay into a rope. They lay the coils next to each other to complete their design. Sometimes, they the clay smooth so the coils do not show. For the slab method, potters flatten the clay into sheets. They the sheets together to make square objects. Sometimes, potters use a wheel to make round objects. To strengthen the pottery, they apply glaze. Glaze in many colors. Finally the pottery goes into an oven, called a kiln. The finished product hard, shiny, and beautiful.

CHAPTER 1

Name ____________________ Date ____________

Lesson 4 Verb Phrases

Teaching

CHAPTER 1

The simple predicate, or verb, may consist of two or more words. These words are called the **verb phrase.** A verb phrase is made up of a main verb and one or more helping verbs.

A main verb can stand by itself as the simple predicate of a sentence.

The Underground Railroad helped slaves.
MAIN VERB (ACTION)

The people involved were brave.
MAIN VERB (LINKING)

Helping verbs help the main verb express action or show time.

Some houses could shelter many slaves at one time.
HELPING VERB

Common Helping Verbs	
Forms of *be*	is, am, was, are, were, be, been
Forms of *do*	do, does, did
Forms of *have*	has, have, had
Others	may, might, can, should, could, would, shall, will

Identifying Verb Phrases

Underline the verb phrase in each sentence. Include main verbs and helping verbs.

1. The Underground Railroad has played a special role in our history.
2. No one really was hidden underground.
3. A network of sympathetic people would help slaves to freedom.
4. These people were called conductors.
5. The hiding places along the way to freedom were called stations.
6. Runaway slaves could stop at the stations for food and clothing.
7. Conductors might show the slaves the best routes to Canada.
8. Many people today are researching the history of the Underground Railroad.
9. Some can follow the routes of the runaway slaves.
10. Most slaves did escape through Ohio, Indiana, and Pennsylvania.
11. Interested history buffs may study the lives of some conductors of the railroad.
12. One famous conductor has been called the "president of the railroad."
13. Levi Coffin may have helped more than 3,000 slaves to freedom.
14. More information will increase our understanding of this period in our history.
15. Do you know any other facts about the Underground Railroad?

Name ______________________________ Date ______________

Verb Phrases

More Practice

A. Identifying Main Verbs and Helping Verbs

Underline the main verb once and the helping verb twice in each of the following sentences.

EXAMPLE Our class is studying about the Underground Railroad.

1. The Underground Railroad was operating in the mid-1800s.
2. Thousands of people were helped to freedom.
3. Many runaway slaves would walk all night.
4. During the day they might be seen by other people.
5. Most slaves had escaped with little food or clothing.
6. Without a guide, they could lose their way to the North.
7. A slave could encounter natural barriers such as rivers or lakes.
8. Stories have been written about the dangerous trip to freedom.
9. Have you read about the Underground Railroad?
10. Do you understand its importance?

B. Writing Verb Phrases

Add a helping verb to complete the verb phrase in each sentence below.

1. Sarah ______________ reading about the Underground Railroad.
2. ______________ you ever hear of Harriet Tubman?
3. It ______________ have been frightening to escape from slavery.
4. The trip to Canada must ______________ been full of danger.
5. ______________ a slave be sure that a hiding place was safe?
6. ______________ you have had the courage to be part of the Underground Railroad?
7. Today we ______________ hardly imagine slavery.
8. Slavery ______________ been gone from America for over 150 years.
9. We ______________ thank the conductors of the Underground Railroad.
10. History books ______________ never forget the conductors' willingness to help others.

CHAPTER 1

Name ______________________ Date ____________

Lesson 4

Verb Phrases

Application

A. Writing Sentences Using Verb Phrases

Make a verb phrase by adding a helping verb to each main verb below. Then write a sentence using the verb phrase. Underline the verb phrase in your sentence.

EXAMPLE jump
Ray will jump over the hurdle in the race.

1. discover
____

2. escape
____

3. search
____

4. help
____

5. swim
____

6. fight
____

B. Writing Using Verb Phrases

Use at least five of the following verb phrases in a story. Write the story on the lines below and underline the verb phrases that you have used. If you like, you can change the tense of the verbs in your paragraph.

will climb	have gone	may find	is working
do remember	has met	would begin	can write

____

____

____

____

____

____

____

____

CHAPTER 1

Name ______________________ Date ____________

Lesson 5

Compound Sentence Parts

Teaching

A **compound subject** is made up of two or more subjects that share the same verb. The subjects are joined by a conjunction, or connecting word, such as *and, or,* or *but.*

Rain and hail fell during the thunderstorm.

COMPOUND SUBJECT

A compound verb is made up of two or more verbs that share the same subject. The verbs are joined by a conjunction such as *and, or,* or *but.*

Snow swirled and drifted into huge mounds.

SUBJECT COMPOUND VERB

CHAPTER 1

Identifying Compound Sentence Parts

In each sentence, underline the words in the compound subject or the compound verb. Do not underline the conjunctions that join the words. On the line to the right, write **CS** for compound subject or **CV** for compound verb.

1. Dark clouds and strong winds were the first sign of the thunderstorm. ____________

2. The brisk winds tossed and turned the small sailboat back and forth. ____________

3. Suddenly, rain and hail pelted the ground. ____________

4. The large hailstones dented or flattened several items in the garden. ____________

5. Lightning flashed and struck a nearby tree. ____________

6. Branches and twigs scattered everywhere. ____________

7. Loud thunder rumbled and crackled overhead. ____________

8. Frightened birds and animals scurried for shelter. ____________

9. An old garbage can bumped and clattered down the street. ____________

10. Luckily, neither my dog nor my cat was outside in the storm. ____________

11. Slender trees bent and swayed in the howling wind. ____________

12. A waterspout damaged or destroyed a few boats in the harbor. ____________

13. No twister or tornado was spotted on land. ____________

14. Some homes and stores were slightly damaged by the strong wind. ____________

15. Finally, the thunder and lightning moved eastward. ____________

16. Raindrops gleamed and glistened as the sun appeared once more. ____________

17. Small puddles and deep pools of water covered the ground. ____________

18. Travis cut and removed the damaged tree. ____________

Name ______________________________ Date ______________

Compound Sentence Parts

More Practice

CHAPTER 1

A. Identifying Simple Subjects and Verbs

In the following sentences underline the subjects once and the verbs twice.

EXAMPLE The thunder crashed and then died away.

1. A tornado damages or destroys everything in its path.
2. Warm, humid air rises and then rotates in a tornado.
3. Powerful winds lift and carry heavy objects long distances.
4. Large trees or even railroad cars can fly through the air like toys.
5. Sensitive weather instruments predict and track these vicious storms.

B. Using Compound Subjects and Compound Verbs

Combine the sentence pairs to form a new sentence with the sentence part in parentheses. Use the conjunction—*and, or, nor,* or *but—that* makes the most sense.

EXAMPLE The road was snow covered. Our driveway was snow covered too. (compound subject)
The road and our driveway were snow covered.

1. The freezing rain caused many accidents. Sleet also caused accidents. (compound subject)

____

2. Snow was falling all night. It was drifting all night too. (compound verb)

____

3. Ian could shovel the snow from the sidewalk. He could sweep the snow from the sidewalk instead. (compound verb)

____

4. Cars were stuck in the deep snow. Trucks were stuck in the deep snow too. (compound subject)

____

5. After the snowfall, Bridget went cross-country skiing. Donna also went cross-country skiing. (compound subject)

____

6. Hot chocolate tasted especially good that day. Homemade cookies tasted good too. (compound subject)

____

Name ________________________ Date ____________

Compound Sentence Parts

Application

A. Sentence Combining with Compound Subjects and Compound Verbs

Write sentences using these compound subjects and compound verbs.

1. ice and snow

____

2. ran and played

____

3. slipped and slid

____

4. wind and rain

____

5. designed and built

____

B. More Sentence Combining

Revise the following paragraph, using compound subjects and compound verbs to combine sentences with similar ideas. Write the new paragraph on the lines below.

A hurricane is a very dangerous storm. Strong winds rip up buildings. These winds blow down buildings too. The whirling wind destroys beaches. High waves destroy beaches also. Huge waves may cause flooding. Heavy rains also cause flooding. People must take shelter away from the path of the storm. Animals also must take shelter from the path of the storm. Hurricane forecasters study the storms. These forecasters track the storms too. Satellites help the forecasters follow the path of the hurricane. Radar helps the forecasters follow the path as well.

____

____

____

____

____

____

____

____

____

CHAPTER 1

Name ______________________________ Date ______________

Lesson 6

Kinds of Sentences

Teaching

CHAPTER 1

A **declarative sentence** expresses a statement. It always ends with a period.

Australia is both a country and a continent.

An **interrogative sentence** asks a question. It always ends with a question mark.

Is Australia the smallest continent?

An **imperative sentence** tells or asks someone to do something. It usually ends with a period but may end with an exclamation point.

Find Australia on this map of the world.

An **exclamatory sentence** shows strong feeling. It always ends with an exclamation point.

I'd love to visit Australia!

Identifying Kinds of Sentences

On the line, identify each sentence below by writing **D** for declarative, **INT** for interrogative, **IMP** for imperative, or **E** for exclamatory. Add the proper punctuation mark at the end of each sentence.

1. Australia is the home of some very unusual animals ______

2. Have you ever heard of the platypus ______

3. What a strange creature it is ______

4. Look for a picture of the platypus in an encyclopedia ______

5. Is the koala a native of Australia ______

6. Koalas like to eat the leaves of the eucalyptus tree ______

7. How cute and cuddly they seem ______

8. Wallabies look like small kangaroos ______

9. List three ways the two animals are different ______

10. Notice how fast the kangaroos run ______

11. Do you know what a dingo is ______

12. A dingo is a wild dog that lives in Australia ______

13. Its howling sends shivers down your spine ______

14. Can you name two Australian birds ______

15. Search for information about the emu and the kookaburra ______

Name ______________________ Date ____________

Kinds of Sentences

More Practice

CHAPTER 1

Using Different Kinds of Sentences

Add the correct end punctuation to each of these sentences. Then rewrite the sentences according to the instructions in parentheses. You may have to add or delete words and change word order.

EXAMPLE How strange those animals are!
(Change to a declarative sentence.)
Those animals are strange.

1. Can you recognize the duck-billed platypus
(Change to a declarative sentence.)

____

2. Tell me where Australia is located
(Change to an interrogative sentence.)

____

3. The capital of Australia is Canberra
(Change to an interrogative sentence.)

____

4. Is the kangaroo out of control
(Change to an exclamatory sentence.)

____

5. What a close call that was
(Change to a declarative sentence.)

____

6. Will you tell us about Australia's history
(Change to an imperative sentence.)

____

7. How dry and barren this land is
(Change to a declarative sentence.)

____

Name ______________________ Date ______________

Kinds of Sentences

Application

A. Writing Different Kinds of Sentences in a Speech

Imagine that you are showing a new student around your school. Write a short speech that you might give as you introduce him or her to your school's most important people and places. Use at least one of each kind of sentence: declarative, interrogative, imperative, and exclamatory. Use the correct punctuation at the end of each sentence.

CHAPTER 1

B. Writing Different Kinds of Sentences in a Diary

Imagine that you are going on a long trip to a faraway place such as Australia. Write a diary entry for one day of your journey. Use at least one of each kind of sentence: declarative, interrogative, imperative, and exclamatory. Use the correct punctuation at the end of each sentence.

Name ______________________________ Date ______________

Lesson 7

Subjects in Unusual Order

Teaching

CHAPTER 1

In most **questions,** the subject comes after the verb or between parts of the verb phrase.

Are you ready? Have you packed a bag? (*Have packed* is the verb phrase)
VERB SUBJECT VERB PHRASE SUBJECT

The subject of a **command,** or imperative sentence, is usually *you*. Often, *you* doesn't appear in the sentence because it is implied, or understood.

Get into the car.
VERB (The **implied subject** is *You.*)

In an **inverted sentence,** the subject comes after the verb.

Off on a trip went the happy family.
VERB SUBJECT

In some sentences beginning with the words ***here*** or ***there,*** the subject follows the verb. You find the subject by looking at the words that follow the verb.

Here is the state park. There are many campsites available.
VERB SUBJECT VERB SUBJECT

Finding Subjects and Verbs in Unusual Positions

In the following sentences, underline the simple subject once and the verb or verb phrase twice. If the subject is understood, write **You** in parentheses on the line.

1. Over the hill came a park ranger. ____________

2. Did he help the family with their tent? ____________

3. Was the tent easy to assemble? ____________

4. There were four air mattresses for four people. ____________

5. Start the campfire carefully. ____________

6. Here is the food for our supper. ____________

7. Near our tent stood a large deer. ____________

8. Was the deer alone or with a group? ____________

9. There goes a family of raccoons through the woods. ____________

10. Look at all the stars in the sky tonight. ____________

11. Can you spot the Big Dipper? ____________

12. Here comes an owl above the treetops. ____________

Name ____________________ Date __________

Subjects in Unusual Order

More Practice

A. Writing Sentences

In the following sentences, underline the simple subject once and the verb twice. Then rewrite each sentence so that the subject comes before the verb.

EXAMPLE Through the woods scurried a frightened rabbit.
A frightened rabbit scurried through the woods.

1. Was the family trip to the state park fun?

____

2. Around the campfire sat the entire family.

____

3. Are boats available at that campsite?

____

4. In the deep lake swam many fish.

____

5. Were you sorry when the trip ended?

____

B. Writing Sentences

Rewrite each sentence as an inverted or imperative sentence. You may choose to add *Here* or *There*. Then underline each subject once and each verb twice in your new sentence.

EXAMPLE The sun rose over our campsite.
Over our campsite rose the sun.

1. You can hike through the forest.

____

2. Beautiful wildflowers grew in the meadow.

____

3. Poison ivy is here by this tree.

____

4. You must extinguish the campfire carefully.

____

5. Wading birds live around the lake.

____

CHAPTER 1

Name ____________________ Date ____________

Subjects in Unusual Order

Application

A. Revising Using Different Sentence Orders

The writer of this paragraph decided never to use the usual word order of subject before verb. In all of the paragraph's sentences, the subject is found in an unusual position or is understood. Rewrite the paragraph. Use a variety of sentence orders to improve the paragraph.

Have you ever gone camping with your family? To a state park went my family last weekend. In a tent camped all four of us. There were many interesting things to do. Through the woods hiked the family. There were wildflowers in the meadow. Around our campsite were spotted many wild animals. There were boats to row on the lake. All too soon came the time to leave. Reluctantly packed my family. To come back to the state park again was our decision.

____

____

____

____

____

____

B. Revising Using a Variety of Sentence Orders

The writer of this paragraph decided always to use the usual word order of subject before verb. Rewrite the paragraph, this time using many kinds of sentence orders. Write at least two sentences in which the subject comes before the verb. Write at least two sentences in a more unusual order, with the subject after the verb.

We made a list of camping equipment to take with us. A tent was first on our list. Air mattresses were also on our list. We included sleeping bags for each of us. A small propane stove for cooking our meals was needed, too. Two large coolers were added to our list. We took enough food and beverages for the entire weekend. Flashlights were at the bottom of the list. Everyone brought some rain gear, just in case. We were ready for anything.

____

____

____

____

____

____

Name ______________________________ Date ______________

Lesson 8

Complements: Subject Complements

Teaching

CHAPTER 1

A complement is a word or group of words that completes the meaning of the verb.

A **subject complement** is a word or group of words that follows a linking verb and renames or describes the subject. Common **linking verbs** include forms of *be,* such as *am, is, are, was,* and *were;* and verbs such as *appear, feel, look, sound, seem,* and *taste.*

Subject complements can act as nouns or adjectives.

A **predicate noun** follows a linking verb and defines or renames the subject.

That dance is the waltz. (*is* is the linking verb)
SUBJECT — dance; PREDICATE NOUN — waltz

A **predicate adjective** follows a linking verb and describes the subject, telling what qualities it has.

The dancers are graceful.
SUBJECT — dancers; PREDICATE ADJECTIVE — graceful

Identifying Linking Verbs and Subject Complements

In the following sentences, underline the linking verbs once and the subject complements twice. On the line, write **PA** for predicate adjective or **PN** for predicate noun.

1. Dancing is one of the oldest forms of communication. ______
2. Dancing is movement in rhythm, usually accompanied by music. ______
3. Ballet is a form of formal dancing performed for audiences. ______
4. Oriental dances are very traditional. ______
5. The square dance, the Irish jig, and the polka are well-known folk dances. ______
6. The dance numbers in movie musicals look imaginative. ______
7. Ballroom dancing appears elegant. ______
8. The tango is a popular Latin-American dance. ______
9. Many dances seem popular for only a short time. ______
10. The waltz became quite fashionable in the 1800s. ______
11. In the 1920s, the Charleston was a fad. ______
12. In the 1930s and 1940s, the swing music of big bands was a big craze. ______
13. The favorite dance of many people in that era was the jitterbug. ______
14. The dances of the 1960s became quite free. ______
15. Dancing remains a popular activity at many celebrations. ______

Name ______________________ Date ____________

Complements: Subject Complements

More Practice

A. Identifying Types of Subject Complements

In each of the following sentences, underline the linking verb once and the subject complement twice. Then, in the blank, write **PN** if the subject complement is a predicate noun or **PA** if it is a predicate adjective.

Example The dance floor is crowded. PA

1. Under the twinkling lights, the auditorium looked magical. ________
2. Ginny is a great dancer. ________
3. Gary seemed nervous before the dance. ________
4. The tickets to the dance were expensive. ________
5. Mrs. Lopez is a chaperone at the dance. ________
6. The band playing at the dance is a local group. ________
7. At first, the music sounded too loud. ________
8. The second song was a familiar favorite for many of the dancers. ________
9. Dancing in a long line is fun. ________
10. The school dance was a success. ________

B. Using Subject Complements

Complete each sentence below. First complete it with a predicate noun. Then complete it with a predicate adjective.

Example The experiment was a success.
The experiment was dangerous.

1. The scientist is ________________.

   The scientist is ________________.

2. The laboratory was ________________.

   The laboratory was ________________.

3. The scientist's assistant was ________________.

   The scientist's assistant was ________________.

4. The award the scientist earned is ________________.

   The award the scientist earned is ________________.

Name ______________________ Date ____________

Lesson 8

Complements: Subject Complements

Application

CHAPTER 1

A. Writing Subject Complements

Rewrite each of the numbered sentences in the passage below with a new subject complement. Underline your new subject complement. If it is a predicate noun, write **PN** in parentheses after the sentence. If it is a predicate adjective, write **PA.**

(1) The dance performance was incredible. **(2)** The dancers seemed confident. **(3)** The dances were very complex. **(4)** My favorite act was the tap-dancing routine. **(5)** Most of the music in the show sounded familiar. **(6)** The show was one of the best I have ever seen.

1. ______________________
2. ______________________
3. ______________________
4. ______________________
5. ______________________
6. ______________________

B. Writing with Subject Complements

Imagine that you have been to a dance or have seen professional dancers at a performance, and you want to tell a friend about your experience. Write six sentences about the dance. Three of the sentences should have predicate adjectives. Three should have predicate nouns.

1. ______________________
2. ______________________
3. ______________________
4. ______________________
5. ______________________
6. ______________________

Name ______________________ Date ______________

Lesson 9

Complements: Objects of Verbs

Teaching

CHAPTER 1

Action verbs often need complements called direct objects and indirect objects to complete their meaning.

A **direct object** is a word or a group of words that names the receiver of the action of an action verb. It answers the question *what?* or *whom?*

Brooke threw the ball. (*What* did Brooke throw?)

An **indirect object** is a word or group of words that tells *to what, to whom,* or *for whom* an action is done. The indirect object usually comes between the verb and the direct object. Verbs that are often followed by an indirect object include *ask, bring, give, hand, lend, make, offer, send, show, teach, tell,* and *write.*

Brooke threw Nicole the ball. (To *whom* did Brooke throw the ball?)

Recognizing Objects of Verbs

In each sentence, if the underlined word is a direct object, write **DO** on the line. If it is an indirect object, write **IO.**

EXAMPLE Ms. Steinberg needed a new compass. *DO*

1. The sparrow chased a big crow from the apple tree. ________
2. We saw a picture of Harriet Tubman in the library. ________
3. The school mailed the new students their registration forms. ________
4. Every year Juan gives the children presents. ________
5. Kings ruled the early Sumerian cities. ________
6. The accident taught the sailors an important lesson. ________
7. My mother bought our family a new computer. ________
8. The wrestling coach told the team the rules. ________
9. Mr. Thies argued the case in court. ________
10. The cocker spaniel waved his bushy tail. ________
11. Give that nail a good whack. ________
12. Will you show the electrician the location of the fuse box? ________
13. Mix a batch of granola for tomorrow's breakfast. ________
14. Alex asked Judith about her knowledge of reptiles. ________
15. Some horses give trainers many problems. ________

Name ______________________ Date __________

Complements: Objects of Verbs

More Practice

A. Identifying Objects of Verbs

Identify the function of the boldfaced word in each sentence below. Write **DO** for direct object and **IO** for indirect object. If the word is not the direct object or the indirect object write **N.**

1. Our visit to the museum was **educational.** __________

2. The tour guide showed our **class** the newest exhibits. __________

3. She patiently answered our **questions.** __________

4. Then, she handed **us** maps of the museum. __________

5. The natural history exhibit was our **favorite.** __________

6. The ancient fossils amazed **everyone.** __________

7. The size of the dinosaur bones surprised **me.** __________

8. The class also enjoyed the rock **exhibit.** __________

9. Some students bought their **families** souvenirs. __________

10. The museum is so big, we could not see **everything.** __________

B. Using Indirect Objects

Underline the direct object in each sentence below. Then rewrite each sentence, adding an indirect object. Use a different indirect object for every sentence.

1. For my mother's birthday, I bought a card.

____

2. My sister did a favor.

____

3. The artist showed his paintings.

____

4. The coach gave some advice.

____

5. The fable taught a lesson about hard work.

____

CHAPTER 1

Name ______________________ Date ____________

Lesson 9

Complements: Objects of Verbs

Application

CHAPTER 1

A. Using Objects of Verbs

Choose one word from each list below to complete each sentence. Use each word only once. Each sentence should have both an indirect object and a direct object. If you wish, you can add words to make the sentences more interesting.

Use as Indirect Object	Use as Direct Object
the jury	some peanuts
the student	a pencil
the audience	the facts of the case
me	a story
the elephant	a letter
the little children	a box of nails
his mother	an A on her essay
the carpenter	a few tricks

1. The magician showed ______________________.

2. The construction worker handed ______________________.

3. The teacher gave ______________________.

4. The zookeeper brought ______________________.

5. The librarian read ______________________.

6. The lawyer told ______________________.

7. The soldier sent ______________________.

8. My friend loaned ______________________.

B. Writing Sentences with Objects of Verbs

Complete each sentence with a direct and an indirect object. Use a different direct and indirect object in every sentence.

Example The radio disk jockey offered *listeners a prize.*

1. The kindergartner made ______________________.

2. My sister taught ______________________.

3. The cat brought ______________________.

4. The audience gave ______________________.

5. The witnesses told ______________________.

Name ______________________ Date ____________

Lesson 10

Fragments and Run-Ons

Teaching

Sentence fragments and run-on sentences are writing errors that can make your writing difficult to understand.

A **sentence fragment** is part of a sentence that is written as if it were a complete sentence. A sentence fragment is missing a subject, a predicate, or both.

Fragments Plants in the desert. (missing a predicate)
Must adapt to life. (missing a subject)
Without much water. (missing both)

Revision Plants in the desert must adapt to life without much water.

A **run-on sentence** is two or more sentences written as if they were a single sentence. When you combine two sentences with a conjunction, use a comma before the conjunction.

Run-On Not much rain falls in the desert some animals still live there.

Revision Not much rain falls in the desert, but some animals still live there.

Identifying Sentences, Sentence Fragments, and Run-Ons

On the short line to the right of each word group below, write **CS, F,** or **RO** to identify the word group as a complete sentence, a fragment, or a run-on sentence.

1. A region that receives little water. ______
2. Months may pass between rainfalls when storms do occur, they may be violent. ______
3. The dry desert soil and hardly any water. ______
4. Piles of sand called *dunes* cover parts of the desert. ______
5. The desert is very hot during the day, the temperature in the desert may drop below freezing at night. ______
6. Animals and plants live in the desert they have developed ways to survive in the hot, dry climate. ______
7. The lives of many desert creatures of the desert. ______
8. Hide in burrows and beneath rocks. ______
9. Desert mammals become active at night. ______
10. Desert reptiles appear at sunrise. ______
11. Desert plants also face the problem of collecting water, the cactus is an expert at holding on to water. ______
12. Need to absorb as much water as possible. ______
13. Not many people except those in the desert. ______

Name ______________________ Date ____________

Fragments and Run-Ons

More Practice

CHAPTER 1

A. Identifying and Correcting Fragments and Run-Ons

On the line after each word group below, write **CS, F,** or **RO** to identify the word group as a complete sentence, a fragment, or a run-on sentence. Then rewrite each fragment or run-on as one or more correct sentences. Add sentence parts as needed.

1. The poster on the wall.

____

2. The photographer took a picture of the beautiful countryside.

____

3. There are shells all over the beach let's collect some.

____

4. Laughed at the comedian's act.

____

5. I love that story I've read it three times.

____

B. Correcting Fragments and Run-Ons

Rewrite this paragraph, correcting each fragment and run-on. You may add words to any fragment to make it a sentence, or combine it with another sentence. To correct a run-on, you may either separate the sentences or join them correctly.

The largest desert in the world. The Sahara in northern Africa. The Sahara covers an area about the size of the United States it extends into ten African countries. Its landscape includes mountains, plateaus, and huge areas of sand. Its population. Less than two million people. The Sahara has a hot, dry climate, some areas have an average rainfall of less than one inch per year.

____

____

____

____

____

____

____

____

____

Name ________________________________ Date ______________

Fragments and Run-Ons *Application*

A. Proofreading for Fragments and Run-Ons

Rewrite this paragraph, correcting each fragment and run-on. You may add words to any fragment to make it a sentence, or combine it with another sentence. To correct a run-on, you may either separate the sentences or join them correctly.

The camel is a large, strong desert animal, camels can travel great distances with little food or water. The camel carries its own food supply. On its back. In the form of a hump. The camel's hump is a large lump of fat the lump provides energy when there is no food. Camels can run about ten miles per hour they can travel as far as one hundred miles in a day they can carry loads up to 330 pounds. Unpredictable behavior. May groan, spit, or kick.

____

____

____

____

____

____

B. Recognizing and Revising Fragments and Run-Ons

Read these notes one student wrote to use in a report. First figure out what the writer was going to say, and then use the information to write a paragraph. Use complete sentences instead of fragments and run-on sentences. Add any words that are needed to make the paragraph understandable.

The chuck wagon. A kitchen on wheels. For cowboys herding cattle in the American West. The word *chuck* means "food" or "grub" that is what was provided at the chuck wagon. The wagon was loaded with food, cooking utensils, and bedding for the cowboys, it was pulled by two teams of horses, it led the way from camp to camp. The cook was one of the most important persons on the trail he was highly paid. Looking after saddles and bridles. Also the cook's job. Many cooks. Quickly feed up to 40 cowboys.

____

____

____

____

____

____

Name ______________________________ Date ______________

Lesson 1

Kinds of Nouns

Teaching

A **noun** is a word that names a person, place, thing, or idea. Examples include *actor, building, ticket,* and *delight.*

A **common noun** is a general name for a person, place, thing, or idea. A **proper noun** is the name of a particular one. For example, *theater* is a common noun; *Palace Theater* is a proper noun. Only proper nouns need to be capitalized.

A **concrete noun** names a thing that can seen, heard, smelled, tasted, or touched. An **abstract noun** names an idea, feeling, quality, or characteristic. For example, *script* and *villain* are concrete nouns, while *excitement* and *dishonesty* are abstract nouns.

A **collective noun** is a word that names a group of people or things, such as *crew.*

CHAPTER 2

A. Identifying Nouns

Underline all the nouns in the following sentences. Every sentence has more than one noun.

1. Julie played the part of the rabbit in the play.

2. Carlos has created beautiful settings with wood and paint.

3. Mrs. Bernard guides the students who are sewing costumes.

4. Do you prefer musical productions or serious plays?

5. Appreciation for the theater begins at home.

B. Identifying Proper and Common Nouns

Underline all the nouns in the following sentences. Write **P** above the proper nouns. Write **C** above the common nouns.

Example A new play (C) opens at the Varieties Theater (P) on Thursday (P).

1. Our class wrote their own play based on the story of King Midas.

2. Children need to use their imaginations watching *Peter Pan.*

3. What a surprise when Peter was pulled up by wires!

4. *The Sound of Music* tells the story of the Trapps, a family of singers.

5. On Friday somebody in the audience created a disturbance.

6. The entire cast wore costumes on Monday.

C. Identifying Types of Nouns

Review the underlined nouns in the sentences in Exercise B. Write the noun requested on the lines below.

1. An abstract noun in sentence 2 ______________________________

2. A concrete noun in sentence 5 ______________________________

3. A collective noun in sentence 6 ______________________________

Name ____________________ Date ____________

Lesson 1

Kinds of Nouns

More Practice

A. Identifying Nouns

Underline all the nouns in each of the following sentences. On the lines below each sentence, write one of the nouns that match the description in parentheses.

1. Gina, was your sister Angela in the play at school?

   (proper) ____________ (common) ____________

2. The audience was amazed by the beauty of the set.

   (concrete) ____________ (abstract) ____________

3. The cast presented a gift to their director, Mrs. Wells.

   (collective) ____________ (proper) ____________

4. Our class gave a special show that was a huge success.

   (collective) ____________ (abstract) ____________

5. As the orchestra took their seats, there was silence.

   (concrete) ____________ (abstract) ____________

B. Using Nouns

Rewrite the following sentences, replacing each boldfaced common noun with a proper noun. Each new noun should reflect the same idea or subject as the boldfaced noun. You may need to change some words, such as *a, an,* or *the,* or delete adjectives.

EXAMPLE The girl at that table lives in a small **town.**
The girl at that table lives in Cherry Valley.

1. The department store closed on the **holiday.**

   ____

2. That **restaurant** serves the best hamburgers.

   ____

3. Our city won an **award** for its flowers.

   ____

4. The train doesn't stop at the next **town.**

   ____

5. My two friends met at the **shopping mall.**

   ____

CHAPTER 2

Name ________________________________ Date ______________

Lesson 1

Kinds of Nouns

Application

A. Using Nouns

Underline all the nouns in each sentence. On the line, write a new sentence using the boldfaced noun.

1. Aunt Shirley suggests that we show more **emotion** in our voices.

____

2. The **committee** gave an award to Mandy Emerson for her performance.

____

3. We need a choreographer for our **dance.**

____

4. Most **audiences** show their enthusiasm with applause.

____

5. Can you hum any **songs** written by George Gershwin?

____

B. Using Nouns

First write one noun of each type listed below. Then write a sentence using the nouns. Underline all the nouns in your sentence.

EXAMPLE common and abstract *children, care*
People who care for children use creativity to keep them busy.

1. collective and proper ______________________________

____

2. proper and abstract ______________________________

____

3. common and concrete ______________________________

____

4. proper and concrete ______________________________

____

5. common and abstract ______________________________

____

CHAPTER 2

Name ______________________________ Date ______________

Lesson 2

Singular and Plural Nouns

Teaching

A **singular noun** names one person, place, thing, or idea. A **plural noun** names more than one person, place, thing, or idea.

One <u>student</u> had an interesting <u>suggestion</u>. (singular nouns)
Several <u>students</u> had interesting <u>suggestions</u>. (plural nouns)

This chart shows the usual ways to form the plurals of nouns.

Singular	Rule	Sample Plural
lamp, table	Add *-s* to most nouns.	lamps, tables
inch, fox	Add *-es* to nouns ending in *s, sh, ch, x,* or *z.*	inches, foxes
radio, stereo	Add *-s* to most nouns that end in *o.*	radios, stereos
echo, hero	Add *-es* to a few nouns that end in *o.*	echoes, heroes
melody, fly monkey, day	Change the *y* to an *i* and add *-es* to most nouns ending in *y.* If a vowel comes before the *y,* add *-s.*	melodies, flies monkeys, days
thief, half roof, cuff	Change the *f* to a *v* and add *-es* to most nouns that end in *f* or *fe.* Add *-s* to a few nouns that end in *f* or *fe.*	thieves, halves roofs, cuffs
corn, tuna	Some nouns keep the same spelling.	corn, tuna
woman, foot	The plural forms of some nouns are irregular.	women, feet

CHAPTER 2

A. Identifying Plural Forms of Nouns

In each sentence, underline only the plural nouns.

1. Most parks have several benches.
2. Students needed to sit to give their feet a rest.
3. The artists brought their sketch pads and pencils.
4. Ellen drew pictures of two deer near some trees.
5. Classes listened to their radios as they ate.
6. Flies buzzed around the bags filled with sandwiches.

B. Correcting Errors in Plural Nouns

In each sentence, the boldfaced plural has been formed incorrectly. Write the correctly spelled plural on the line.

1. My brother and cousin are **freshmans** in high school. ______________
2. Their **classs** begin at eight o'clock. ______________
3. Some **dayes** they stay late for band practice. ______________
4. One day they went looking for **mysterys** at the library. ______________
5. The high **shelfs** had books by their favorite author. ______________
6. Brad reached them easily because he is six **feets** tall. ______________

Name ______________________________ Date ______________

Singular and Plural Nouns

More Practice

A. Identifying Plural Forms of Nouns

In each sentence, underline only the plural nouns.

1. We help the women in the cafeteria on Mondays.
2. Terry and I use brushes to clean the vegetables.
3. Potatoes and carrots both need scrubbing.
4. Fresh loaves of bread are delivered on trays.
5. The sandwiches we make are called heroes.
6. French fries are one of the most popular foods in school cafeterias.

CHAPTER 2

B. Correcting Errors in Plural Nouns

In each sentence, find and underline the plural that has been formed incorrectly. Write the correctly spelled plural on the line.

1. Some communitys have ethnic food-tasting events. ______________
2. It's fun to taste dishs from countries around the world. ______________
3. The womens in Mom's club hold food fairs every year. ______________
4. Tables and chaires are set up near the fieldhouse. ______________
5. Our family donates boxs of paper goods. ______________
6. Sharp knifes were needed to cut the pizzas. ______________
7. They try to keep the childrens busy with games. ______________
8. Eight mans entertained guests with country music. ______________
9. The melodys were familiar to most of the guests. ______________
10. A few senior citizens sat in the shade under tree branchs. ______________

C. Using Plural Nouns

Form the plural of the given nouns. Then use all three plurals in a single sentence.

1. woman ______________ costume ______________ dance ______________

____

____

2. party ______________ home ______________ sandwich ______________

____

____

Name ______________________________ Date ______________

Lesson 2

Singular and Plural Nouns

Application

A. Identifying and Using Plural Nouns

In the following sentences, decide whether each noun is in the correct form, singular or plural. If the noun should be plural, has the plural been formed correctly? Rewrite every sentence with the correct noun forms.

1. One of my favorite activitys is being on the debating team.

2. They meet two Monday a month, except for two summer month.

3. I get tired when I stand on my feets for more than two houres.

4. Last week two classs debated: "Should we stop trading with some countrys?"

5. A women from the mayor's office gave two speechs at our school.

6. She said we need to prepare to be good citizenes.

7. One boys said there should be more heros in government service.

8. We could send faxs to our state senatores.

B. Using Nouns

You are setting up a poster display in a city park to teach about the animals and plants of your area. Write a short paragraph telling which animals and plants you want to write about and why. Underline at least five plural nouns in your paragraph.

CHAPTER 2

Name ______________________ Date ____________

Possessive Nouns

Teaching

The possessive form of a noun shows ownership or relationship. Use an apostrophe and *-s* to show possession. For example, *wren's nest* (ownership); *Mom's friend* (relationship).

You may use possessive nouns in place of longer phrases.

Everybody met at the front gate of the museum.
Everybody met at the museum's front gate.

The following chart shows the usual ways to form the plurals of possessive nouns.

Noun	Rule		Possessive
Singular:	bird	Add an apostrophe and *-s*	bird's family
Plural ending in *-s:*	eggs	Add an apostrophe	eggs' colors
Plurals not ending in *-s:*	men	Add an apostrophe and *-s*	men's hats

CHAPTER 2

A. Identifying Possessive Nouns

Underline each possessive noun. On the blank, write **S** if that noun is singular or **P** if it is plural.

1. Mrs. Cass's class took several field trips this year. ______
2. Their science unit's subject was animal homes. ______
3. Which trees' branches seem to attract more birds? ______
4. Karl's idea was to take pictures of some bird eggs. ______
5. Three students' cameras already had film in them. ______

B. Using Possessive Nouns

Complete each sentence with the possessive form of the word shown in parentheses.

1. Two ______________ backpacks were left in the picnic area. (children)
2. My ______________ notebook got wet in the rain. (friend)
3. In one tree we saw evidence of a ______________ home. (woodpecker)
4. ______________ tape recorder came in handy. (Lisa)
5. We all kept quiet when she recorded some baby ______________ chirps. (robins)

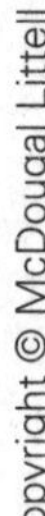

C. Using Possessives in Phrases

Rewrite the sentences, changing the boldfaced phrases to possessives.

1. The **reports of students** will be due next Friday morning.

____

2. David decided to compare **the nests of two birds.**

____

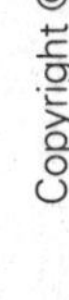

Name ________________________________ Date ____________

Lesson 3

Possessive Nouns

More Practice

A. Identifying Possessive Nouns

Underline each possessive noun in these sentences. On the blank, write **S** for singular and **P** for plural. There are two possessives in each sentence.

1. Pigeons' roosts were on our building's window ledge. ______
2. In a year's time, I saw many pigeons' eggs in our flowerpots. ______
3. It was the owner's decision to remove my mother's pots. ______
4. Because of Mom's love of birds, we borrowed the Smiths' bird feeder. ______
5. We can't see the pigeons' roosts anymore, but we hope each bird's hunger is satisfied. ______

CHAPTER 2

B. Correcting Errors in Possessive Nouns

In each sentence, find and underline the possessive that has been formed incorrectly. Write the correctly spelled possessive on the line.

1. Citie's skyscrapers are home to many birds. ______
2. In Baltimore, a peregrine falcons's nest was found on a roof. ______
3. Many scientist's studies stated that those birds were an endangered species. ______
4. Through many peoples' efforts, the falcon was able to breed. ______
5. In Argentina, several Quaker parakeet's nests are in one tree. ______
6. Up to 12 birds's nests may be in the same tree! ______
7. Some burrowing owls's burrows are guarded just like castles. ______
8. An owl at the front of the burrow imitates a sentrys' stance. ______

C. Using Possessives in Sentences

Form a possessive for each noun given. Then use it in a sentence.

1. scientists ______

______

2. citizen ______

______

Name ______________________ Date __________

Possessive Nouns

Application

A. Correcting Errors in Possessive Nouns

Check the boldfaced possessive nouns in these sentences. If the possessive is formed incorrectly, write the correct form on the blank. If it is correct, write **C.**

1. **Sams'** sketches are displayed near the school office. __________
2. It is a good way to compare several **birds'** habitats. __________
3. Most cliff **swallows's** nests are made of mud pellets. __________
4. You can observe their nests on a cliff or under a **buildings'** eaves. __________
5. Some **student's** reports are about the diets of various birds. __________
6. I read that a bald **eagles'** favorite food is salmon. __________
7. Victor taped the sound made by a **hummingbird's** wings. __________
8. Some **birds's** migration journeys can cover thousands of miles. __________
9. The **map's** key can help you figure the distance in miles. __________
10. On **Parents'** Night, we will present our bird projects. __________

B. Using Possessive Nouns in Sentences

Change each set of words in parentheses into a possessive phrase. Write a sentence using that phrase.

EXAMPLE (wings of the bird) *bird's wing*
The bird's wings had been clipped.

1. (interest of the children) __________
2. (visiting hours at the hospital) __________
3. (hobbies of my friend) __________
4. (speech of the museum guide) __________

CHAPTER 2

Name ______________________________ Date ______________

Compound Nouns

Teaching

A **compound noun** is made up of two or more words used together as a single noun.

You might see compound nouns written in one of three ways:

One single word: *rooftop*
Two or more separate words: *window shade*
A hyphenated word: *brother-in-law*

The following chart shows the usual ways to form the plurals of compound nouns.

Singular	Rule		Plural
One word	townhouse mailbox	Add *-s* to most words Add *-es* to words that end in *ch, sh, s,* or *x.*	townhouses mailboxes
Two or more words or hyphenated words	wind chime straw in the wind eight-year-old lady-in-waiting	Make the main noun plural. The main noun is the noun that is modified.	wind chimes straws in the wind eight-year-olds ladies-in-waiting

A. Identifying Compound Nouns

Underline every compound noun in the following sentences.

1. The farmhouse of my great-uncle was being remodeled.
2. Summertime is my favorite season to spend weekends together.
3. I helped my uncle build a new henhouse and pigsty.
4. Dad let me use tools like the screwdriver and handsaw.
5. The mailbox and lawn mower needed fixing.

B. Using Plural Compound Nouns

Underline compound nouns that are incorrectly spelled. Rewrite the sentences, using the correct plural form of those nouns.

1. The messiest job was cleaning the paintbrushs.

   ____

2. When I finished nailing wallboardes, I went out to the back yard.

   ____

3. Morning glorys were climbing up the sides of the fence.

   ____

4. My two greats-aunt, Lucy and Helen, carried kitchen utensils outdoors.

   ____

5. They asked me to wash some breadboxs with a hose.

   ____

Name ______________________ Date ______________

Lesson 4

Compound Nouns

More Practice

A. Identifying Compound Nouns

Underline every compound noun in these sentences. Above each compound noun, write **S** for singular or **P** for plural. Notice that each sentence has two compound nouns.

1. Our mail carrier brought me a letter that made me as excited as a bag of jumping beans!
2. My great-grandmother sent me an airplane ticket.
3. She's in a wheelchair because of her recent heart attack.
4. The airport was near the Twin Cities in Minnesota.
5. I was welcomed with bear hugs, muffins, and a glass of root beer.
6. How surprised I was to see her two sisters-in-law in the dining room!
7. They were setting some teaspoons on beautiful placemats.

B. Using Compound Nouns

Write the plural forms for each set of compound words. Then use all three plural compounds in a single sentence.

1. baked bean ______________

   hot dog ______________

   paper plate ______________

   ____

2. bluebird ______________

   sunflower ______________

   window box ______________

   ____

3. brother-in-law ______________

   snowman ______________

   wristwatch ______________

   ____

CHAPTER 2

Name ______________________ Date ____________

Lesson 4

Compound Nouns

Application

A. Identifying Compound Nouns

Underline two or more compound nouns in each sentence. Then rewrite the sentences, changing the singular compounds to plurals. The words in parentheses can be deleted.

Example My grandparent had a reunion with (a) schoolmate.
My grandparents had a reunion with schoolmates.

1. The girlfriend acted as bridesmaid at their wedding.

____

2. In those days it was common for (an) eighteen-year-old to be (a) newlywed.

____

3. Their brother-in-law, the groomsman, had the job of giving out (a) place card.

____

4. Lily-of-the-valley made (a) beautiful centerpiece on the tabletop.

____

5. For brunch they ate (a) pancake, (a) ladyfinger, and (a) blueberry.

____

6. The wedding gifts included (a) teapot, (an) ironing board, and (a) doormat.

____

B. Using Compound Nouns in Writing

Write a compound noun for each phrase listed below. Then use these compounds in a paragraph telling about an unusual or scary dream. Let your imagination take over.

Example a fence with chain links *a chain-link fence*

bill worth twenty dollars ______________

bowl for fish ______________

paper with news ______________

____

____

____

____

____

____

CHAPTER 2

Name ________________________________ Date ______________

Lesson 5

Nouns and Their Jobs

Teaching

In sentences, **nouns** have different jobs.

As the **subject,** a noun tells who or what the sentence is about.

Brian is getting ready for a baseball game. His **team** is in first place.

As the **complement,** a noun completes the meaning of the verb. This chart shows how a noun may work as a **predicate noun,** a **direct object,** and an **indirect object.**

Predicate noun	renames or defines the subject after a linking verb	My sister is the **captain.**
Direct object	names the receiver of the action of the action verb	Hector kicked the **football.**
Indirect object	tells *to whom* or *what* or *for whom* or *what* an action is done	The coach gave the **team** their awards.

A noun or pronoun that follows a preposition is the **object of the preposition.**

My uncle ran in the **marathon**. He competed for the **trophy**.

Identifying Subjects, Complements, and Objects of Prepositions

In each sentence, identify the word in bold type. On the blank, write **S** for subject, **PN** for predicate noun, **O** for object, **DO** for direct object, or **OP** for object of the preposition.

1. Nancy was the **goalie** for Monday's soccer game. ______
2. She threw the **ball** across the field. ______
3. Mr. Rollins gave the **student** a message for his parents. ______
4. He is the **teacher** in charge of bus transportation. ______
5. Our **class** sent the senator an invitation. ______
6. Our boat was severely damaged by **rocks.** ______
7. Mrs. Chin made **appetizers** for the reception. ______
8. Her son Robert was **president** of our class this year. ______
9. In the **winter,** bowling is Greg's favorite activity. ______
10. To save time, Coach Elliott gave the **team** their uniforms. ______
11. **New York City** is a city known for its sports teams. ______
12. Our friends carried **cushions** to sit on. ______
13. How many laps did Sandy swim at your **pool?** ______

Name ________________________ Date ____________

Lesson 5

Nouns and Their Jobs

More Practice

A. Identifying Nouns as Complements

Underline the subject of each sentence. Then identify the complement in bold type. Write **PN** for predicate noun, **DO** for direct object, or **IO** for indirect object.

1. Dan will show the **visitor** the location of the lockers. ______

2. Today's goalie was the newest **person** on the soccer team. ______

3. The accident taught the swimmers an important **lesson.** ______

4. Our wrestling coach told the **players** the rules and regulations. ______

5. Vicky is a **manager** at Dad's health club. ______

6. Marty leads the **league** in home runs. ______

7. Ms. Casali mailed the new **students** registration forms. ______

8. The principal found my brother a summer **job.** ______

9. My uncle bought our **family** season tickets for the baseball games. ______

10. For two years Ronnie has been **treasurer** of the league. ______

B. Using Nouns as Objects of Prepositions

Underline every prepositional phrase in the sentences. On the blanks that follow, write each noun that is an object of the preposition.

EXAMPLE: There were several players chosen for the tournament. *tournament*

1. The bicycle in the garage has had a flat tire for two weeks.

______ ______

2. Before class Lindsay did 50 sit-ups on the gym mat.

______ ______

3. Outside the stadium, loyal fans lined up by the box office.

______ ______

4. We saw a picture of Babe Ruth in that magazine.

______ ______

5. Can we jog among the walkers at the park?

______ ______

CHAPTER 2

Name ______________________ Date ____________

Lesson 5

Nouns and Their Jobs

Application

A. Identifying Nouns Used as Complements

Underline each subject in the following sentences. Then identify every boldfaced word as a predicate noun **(PN),** a direct object **(DO),** or an indirect object **(IO).**

1. My cousin entered this year's **Special Olympics.** ______
2. Some horses give **trainers** many problems. ______
3. Baxter Junior College offered Dana a **scholarship.** ______
4. Last summer Mom gave **Phil** a mitt for his birthday. ______
5. Clarise wrote Sam a **letter** about her vacation. ______
6. The whole outdoors was our **classroom** for the day. ______
7. Juan was our **guide** for the annual Open House. ______
8. Parents brought the **teachers** a platter of cookies. ______

B. Using Nouns as Objects of Prepositions

For each phrase, write a noun as the object of the preposition. Then write a sentence using the entire phrase.

1. under a ______________

____

2. into the ______________

____

3. beyond the ______________

____

4. across the ______________

____

5. down the ______________

____

CHAPTER 2

Name ______________________________ Date ______________

What Is a Pronoun?

Teaching

A **pronoun** is a word that is used in place of a noun or another pronoun. The word that a personal pronoun refers to is called its **antecedent.**

Personal pronouns, such as *I, we, he,* and *them,* change their forms to reflect **person, number,** and **case.**

Person Personal pronouns have different forms for first person, second person, and third person.

Number Pronouns can be singular or plural.

Case Personal pronouns change their forms depending on how they are used in a sentence. Each pronoun has three cases: subject, object, and possessive.

Personal Pronouns

		Subject	Object	Possessive
Singular	***First Person***	I	me	my, mine
	Second Person	you	you	your, yours
	Third Person	he, she, it	him, her, it	his, her, hers, its
Plural	***First Person***	we	us	our, ours
	Second Person	you	you	your, yours
	Third Person	they	them	their, theirs

Finding Personal Pronouns

Underline each personal pronoun in the following sentences.

1. My favorite vacation is a trip to Williamsburg.
2. Williamsburg is a special place that reflects our colonial history.
3. You feel as though you are living long ago.
4. The people dress the way they did in colonial times.
5. Ladies wear their long skirts and gowns.
6. Men carry three-cornered hats with them.
7. You might watch a cook as she stirs her stew at the fireplace.
8. Candlelight casts its soft glow over the kitchen.
9. You may notice a coachman as he moves his coach skillfully down the street.
10. Several taverns allow us to sample colonial food.
11. They use recipes from the early settlers.
12. Your family can listen to music played on unusual instruments.
13. We can try our luck at tooting a tin whistle.
14. To me, touring the Governor's Mansion is a treat.
15. Think about visiting it sometime.

Name ____________________ Date ____________

Lesson 1

What Is a Pronoun?

More Practice

A. Finding Personal Pronouns

Underline each personal pronoun in the following sentences.

1. Have you ever been to Jamestown?
2. It was the first permanent English settlement in our country.
3. The first colonists were men and boys who thought they would find gold.
4. Their dream of finding treasure never came true.
5. A man had to use all his skills just to survive.
6. Life was very hard for them.
7. When women joined the colony, they brought other skills with them.
8. They tended the garden and preserved its produce.
9. A mother would teach her children to read and write.
10. She would spin and weave to make cloth.
11. Each child had his or her chores to do.
12. Perhaps a child would help his or her mother in the family garden.
13. He or she might help make candles.
14. Parents then, just like parents now, had high hopes for their children.
15. Jamestown is a special place for us.

B. Using Personal Pronouns

Replace the underlined nouns in this paragraph with personal pronouns. Write the pronouns on the lines below.

Squanto was a Pawtuxet Indian man who came to the aid of the Pilgrims at Plymouth Colony. The **(1)** Pilgrims were near starvation after a very bad winter. Squanto taught the **(2)** Pilgrims how to plant corn. **(3)** Squanto showed the Pilgrims the best places to hunt and fish. **(4)** Squanto's ability to speak English came in quite handy for the Pilgrims. Squanto acted as the **(5)** Pilgrims' interpreter with the Indian chief Massasoit when the two groups were working out a treaty. **(6)** Squanto proved **(7)** Squanto's friendship with the Pilgrims many times. The **(8)** Pilgrims were grateful.

1. ____________ **5.** ____________

2. ____________ **6.** ____________

3. ____________ **7.** ____________

4. ____________ **8.** ____________

Name ________________________ Date ____________

Lesson 1

What Is a Pronoun?

Application

A. Using Personal Pronouns

Rewrite this paragraph, using personal pronouns to replace some of the nouns that have been used too often. Write your revised paragraph on the lines below.

Food was plentiful in the colonies. Food came from many sources. The colonists grew grains, fruits, and vegetables on the colonists' farms. The colonists raised cattle, hogs, and chickens as well. A man could hunt for wild game in the fields or a man could fish in the river or ocean. Usually, a woman used ground wheat or corn to make bread. A woman selected herbs from a nearby garden. A woman's kitchen was filled with delicious aromas.

B. Using Personal Pronouns in a Diary

Historians tell us what daily life was like in colonial times. Someday, historians will study the everyday events of today too. Write a diary entry for a typical day in your life right now. Be sure to use a variety of personal pronouns.

CHAPTER 3

Name ______________________________ Date ______________

Lesson 2

Subject Pronouns

Teaching

A **subject pronoun** is used as the subject of a sentence or as a predicate pronoun after a linking verb.

Subject Pronouns

Singular	Plural
I	we
you	you
he, she, it	they

Use the **subject case** of a pronoun when the pronoun is the subject of a sentence. Remember that a pronoun can be part of a compound subject.

Subject The Wright brothers liked bicycles. They were also interested in flying. (*They* replaces *The Wright brothers.*)

Part of compound subject Wilbur and he were willing to try almost anything.

Use the subject case for predicate pronouns. A **predicate pronoun** follows a linking verb and renames, or refers to, the subject. Remember that the most common linking verbs are forms of the verb be and include *is, am, are, was, were, been, has been, have been, can be, will be, could be,* and *should be.*

Predicate pronoun Great friends were they.

A. Identifying Subject Pronouns

Underline all the subject pronouns in the following sentences.

1. Even when the Wright brothers were boys, they were interested in mechanics.
2. Did you know that Orville built a printing press?
3. He and Wilbur also made bicycles in their small shop.
4. They became interested in flying after reading about glider pioneer, Otto Lilienthal.
5. Soon it became their primary interest.
6. After Wilbur and Orville's first attempts at flying failed, they did not quit.
7. We have written records about their experiments with airplane wings.

B. Using Subject Pronouns

Underline the correct pronoun to complete each sentence.

1. Although the Wright brothers went to Kitty Hawk in September, (them, they) made their first successful flight in December.
2. When Orville first flew the plane, (him, he) stayed airborne for 12 seconds.
3. At first, (we, us) in America did not pay much attention to this flight.
4. Later, Wilbur and (him, he) made hundreds of flights in their new machine.
5. Living in the age of jets and rockets, you and (me, I) should appreciate the Wright brothers' contributions to flight.

Name ______________________ Date ______________

Lesson 2

Subject Pronouns

More Practice

A. Using Subject Pronouns

In each sentence, underline the pronoun that completes each sentence correctly.

1. (We, Us) know that the idea of flying goes back thousands of years.
2. You and (me, I) have heard the Greek myth about Icarus.
3. His father and (him, he) flew with feather and wax wings.
4. The Chinese invented kites; (they, them) were so large they could lift a person off the ground.
5. In the 1800s (it, its) was considered a milestone when two Frenchmen floated over Paris in a hot air balloon.
6. Inventors worked on gliders, but (they, them) could not carry passengers or cargo.
7. When Samuel P. Langley built a steam-powered airplane, both the pilot and (he, him) were sure it would fly.
8. Unfortunately for Mr. Langley, (us, we) know that the Wright brothers were the first to successfully fly a motor-powered airplane.
9. During the early 1900s airplanes improved; soon (they, them) were traveling great distances.
10. Although Charles Lindbergh made the first nonstop flight across the Atlantic, (he, him) was in the air 33 and one-half hours.
11. Amelia Earhart also flew nonstop across the Atlantic; the first woman to do so was (her, she).

B. Choosing Subject Pronouns

Fill in the blanks in the following sentences with appropriate subject pronouns. Vary the pronouns you use, and do not use the pronoun *you.*

1. May Beth and ______________ help with the decorations?
2. If you ask Paul and Dave, ______________ will be glad to fix your computer.
3. ______________ went to the skating rink with our friends.
4. Are Stephanie and ______________ singing in the school concert?
5. When the streets got wet, ______________ became very slippery.
6. The starting quarterback will be either Marcus or ______________.
7. Brendan and ______________ wrote an interesting report on reptiles.

CHAPTER 3

Name ____________________ Date ____________

Subject Pronouns

Application

A. Proofreading

Proofread the following story to make sure that subject pronouns have been used in the right places. When you find a pronoun used incorrectly, cross it out. Then insert this proofreading symbol ^ and write the correct pronoun above it.

Can you and me imagine what the Wright brothers' first flight was like? Wilbur and Orville had read everything available about airplanes. Wilbur and him had built a wind tunnel and experimented with different types of airplane wings. They had contacted the Weather Bureau to find the ideal place for their trials. When the brothers arrived at Kitty Hawk in September 1903, severe storms and other problems kept them from flying their new airplane. Finally, everything was set. The flight was to be on December 17, 1903. When Orville took off, he flew 120 feet. Taking turns flying three more times that day were Wilbur and him. One of Wilbur's flights was the longest. Only five people watched this first flight of an engine-powered flying machine. Us cannot be sure exactly what happened because the few newspaper stories about the flight were not accurate. However, you and me can be grateful to two mechanically minded brothers from Dayton, Ohio.

B. Using Pronouns in Writing

Imagine that you have just taken a plane trip. On the plane, you saw all kinds of people traveling with you. Write a paragraph about the people you saw on the trip. Be sure to use at least four subject pronouns correctly.

CHAPTER 3

Name ______________________ Date ____________

Lesson 3

Object Pronouns

Reteaching

Object pronouns are personal pronouns used as direct objects, as indirect objects, or as the objects of prepositions.

Singular	Plural
me	us
you	you
him, her, it	them

As a **direct object,** the pronoun receives the action of a verb and answers the question *whom* or *what.* As an **indirect object,** the pronoun tells *to whom or what* or *for whom or what* an action is performed. As an **object of a preposition,** the pronoun follows a preposition such as *to, from, for, against, by, between,* or *about.*

Direct object	People liked P. T. Barnum because he entertained them. (*Whom* did he entertain? *them*)
Indirect object	Barnum showed them fascinating objects. (To *whom* did he show the objects? *them*)
Object of the preposition	Many people worked for him. (*For* is the preposition.)

CHAPTER 3

A. Identifying Object Pronouns

Underline all the object pronouns in the following sentences.

1. P. T. Barnum was a one-of-a-kind person; some called him a showman.
2. Others had a different name for him; they called him a fake.
3. Once, he charged people to see a person he said was George Washington's mother, but he was just fooling them.
4. The woman he showed them had never even seen George Washington or talked to him.
5. Many people happily paid to see her anyway.
6. Barnum not only fooled people; he entertained them.

B. Using Object Pronouns

Underline the correct pronoun to complete each sentence.

1. When P. T. Barnum found Tom Thumb, he asked the little man to work for (he, him).
2. People were delighted with (he, him) because he was only about two feet tall.
3. Barnum told Tom's parents that he would bring (he, him) back home soon.
4. Even people in England were amazed when Barnum showed (they, them) little Tom Thumb.
5. People even paid to see the Feejee Mermaid. No one could believe in (she, her).

Name ______________________________ Date ______________

Lesson 3

Object Pronouns

More Practice

A. Using Object Pronouns

In each sentence, underline the pronoun that completes each sentence correctly.

1. When P. T. Barnum told a lie, it probably made (he, him) rich.
2. People called (he, him) the "Prince of Humbug."
3. Who could believe (him, he) when he said that he had found George Washington's mother?
4. Some cynics said that she was just a robot, and people stopped paying good money to see (her, she).
5. Barnum began to advertise oddities like the "Wild Man of Borneo." How much would you pay to see (he, him)?
6. Barnum never thought people were very smart. He knew that he could fool (they, them) easily.
7. Barnum sewed a monkey's head to a fish's body and called (she, her) the Feejee Mermaid.
8. People actually paid to see (she, her) too.
9. If Barnum had told them he had brought back aliens from Mars, some people probably would have believed (him, he).
10. Most people probably knew Barnum was fooling (they, them).
11. They were glad to pay (he, him) because he made (they, them) laugh and surprised (they, them).

B. Choosing Object Pronouns

Fill in the blanks in the following sentences with appropriate object pronouns. Vary the pronouns you use, and do not use the pronoun *you.*

1. The soldier at the gate saluted Jimmy and ________________.
2. When will you send ________________ the yellow yarn?
3. The host of the party greeted ________________ and ________________ at the door.
4. The stranger asked ________________ for directions.
5. Uncle Irving told ________________ a funny story.
6. Luckily, Jason taught ________________ the Heimlich maneuver.

CHAPTER 3

Name ______________________________ Date ______________

Lesson 3

Object Pronouns

Application

A. Proofreading

The following story contains several errors in the use of object pronouns. As you read, you will probably be able to pick out the errors right away because they sound really wrong. When you find a pronoun used incorrectly, cross it out. Then insert this proofreading symbol ^ and write the correct pronoun above it.

P. T. Barnum was born in 1810. When he grew up, he realized that people needed something to entertain they. So he offered they some strange sights. He decided that they would like to see a tiny person that he had found. Charles Stratton (Barnum renamed he General Tom Thumb) was only five years old when Barnum found him. What was amazing about him was his size. He weighed only about 15 pounds and was less than two feet tall. In the United States and England, people paid to see Tom and marvel at he. With the money Barnum made showing Tom and other acts, he started a circus. He called his circus "The Greatest Show on Earth."

B. Using Object Pronouns in Writing

Imagine yourself at the circus. You would see many people in the acts and in the stands. Write a paragraph about the people you could see on the trip. Use at least five object pronouns in your paragraph.

CHAPTER 3

Name ______________________ Date ______________

Lesson 4

Possessive Pronouns

Teaching

Possessive pronouns are personal pronouns used to show ownership or relationship.

Singular	Plural
my, mine	our, ours
your, yours	your, yours
her, hers, his, its	their, theirs

The possessive pronouns *my, your, her, his, our,* and *their* come before nouns. The possessive pronouns *mine, ours, yours, his, hers,* and *theirs* can stand alone in a sentence.

<u>My</u> future could be exciting.
Some people's ideas of the future are scary. I think <u>mine</u> are interesting.

Some possessive pronouns sound like contractions *(its/it's, your/you're, their/they're).* Don't confuse these pairs. Remember that possessive pronouns never use an apostrophe. Contractions always use an apostrophe.

Contraction <u>It's</u> a dream of mine to travel in the future.
Possessive What will happen to our city? <u>Its</u> future is cloudy.

CHAPTER 3

A. Identifying Possessive Pronouns

Underline all the possessive pronouns in the following sentences.

1. When your great-grandparents were children, space travel was just a dream.
2. By the time their grandchildren were born, satellites were circling Earth.
3. Today, scientists talk of flights to Mars. Would you like to walk on its surface?
4. The exploration of space will be just one exciting element in our future.
5. Iris and Rob are friends of mine.
6. Their images of the future are quite different from each other.
7. In her mind, the best thing about the future is its endless possibilities.
8. His vision of the future includes dangers such as more pollution and crime.
9. How do their visions of the future compare to yours?

B. Using Possessive Pronouns

Underline the correct pronoun or word to complete each sentence. Be careful not to confuse contractions and possessive pronouns.

1. How we see the future tells us something about how we see (our, your) present.
2. (It's, Its) a sure bet that the future will hold surprises we can't imagine today.
3. Jack's family made a time capsule for (their, they're) future grandchildren to see.
4. If you worry too much about (your, you're) future, you may not enjoy the present.
5. Ellen has just won a piano competition, and (her, hers) future looks bright.

Name ______________________________ Date ______________

Lesson 4

Possessive Pronouns

More Practice

A. Using Possessive Pronouns

In each sentence, underline the pronoun or word that completes each sentence correctly.

1. With more than six billion people in the world, (our, ours) future may be crowded.
2. (My, Mine) hope for the future is that we find a cure for cancer.
3. Some people are frightened by the future. They are afraid of (its, it's) uncertainty and (it's, its) dangers.
4. A friend of (my, mine) is eager for the future.
5. She has no doubt about (her, its) role in the 21st century. She is convinced she will be president!
6. Some people believe that (their, they're) chances of living 200 years in the future are excellent.
7. At school last week, a speaker reminded the students that the future was (their, theirs).
8. Sam's vision of the future sounds like a video game. (Yours, your) seems to be more realistic.
9. Carla entered an essay contest about the future. (Hers, Her) was judged to be the best essay on life in the 21st century.
10. In the essay, she shares (her, she) dream of living in an underwater city.
11. Even though you didn't win a prize, (your, you're) painting of the family space shuttle of the future was amazing.
12. We can only imagine robots and computers that do all (our, their) work and thinking for us.

B. Choosing Possessive Pronouns

Fill in the blanks in the following sentences with appropriate possessive pronouns. Vary the pronouns you use.

1. For several days the oriole prepared a nest for ________________ young.
2. Is ________________ latest album out yet?
3. ________________ newspaper was wet, so ________________ pages stuck together.
4. The maple tree lost ________________ leaves.
5. His saddle shoes are newer than ________________.
6. Their national anthem is easier to sing than ________________.

CHAPTER 3

Name ______________________ Date ______________

Lesson 4

Possessive Pronouns

Application

A. Proofreading

Proofread the following story to make sure that possessive pronouns have been used in the right places. When you find a pronoun used incorrectly, cross it out. Then insert this proofreading symbol ^ and write the correct pronoun above it.

In the past, people have imagined what theirs lives would be like in the future. Some of their predictions look funny to us now. Our planet has not been taken over by Martians. People don't spend your days flying in rockets to the moon. The planet has not seen all it's natural beauty destroyed by nuclear war. However, many things that people in the past imagined for ours world today have come true. Helicopters, television, and automobiles were first predicted by science-fiction writers. Jules Verne was one of these writers. He looked at its world and saw its future over 100 years ago. In books such as *Twenty Thousand Leagues Under the Sea* and *From the Earth to the Moon,* he predicted submarines and travel to other planets.

B. Using Possessive Pronouns in Writing

Picture yourself in the future. You will use many new machines and ways of getting around. You will wear different clothes from the ones you wear today. Think of ways in which your life will change and write a paragraph about your life in 50 years. Use at least five possessive pronouns in your paragraph.

CHAPTER 3

Name ______________________________ Date ______________

Lesson 5

Reflexive and Intensive Pronouns

Teaching

Pronouns that end in *-self* or *-selves* are either reflexive or intensive pronouns.

Reflexive and Intensive Pronouns

myself	yourself	herself, himself, itself
ourselves	yourselves	themselves

A **reflexive pronoun** refers to the subject and directs the action of the verb back to the subject. Reflexive pronouns are necessary to the meaning of a sentence. Without them the sentence doesn't make sense.

The climbers warned themselves to be prepared for anything. (*Themselves* refers to *climbers.*)

An **intensive pronoun** emphasized the noun or pronoun within the same sentence. Intensive pronouns are not necessary to the meaning of the sentence.

I myself would like to climb a high mountain someday. (*Myself* refers to *I.*)

Remember that *hisself* and *theirselves* are not real words. Never use them. Use *himself* and *themselves* instead.

CHAPTER 3

A. Identifying Reflexive and Intensive Pronouns

Underline all the reflexive and intensive pronouns in the following sentences.

1. The mountain itself is quite a challenge.
2. He hurt himself while he was climbing.
3. My sister climbed the mountain herself.
4. We started giving ourselves more breaks as we got closer to the top.
5. Tell yourself you can make it to the top.
6. In my dreams, I saw myself climbing the most challenging mountain.

B. Using Reflexive and Intensive Pronouns

Underline the correct pronoun to complete each sentence.

1. When you climb a mountain, you challenge (you, yourself) to accomplish things you didn't think were possible.
2. Every successful climber is proud of (himself or herself, him or her) for facing fear and accomplishing worthwhile goals.
3. Even such excellent climbers as Sir Edmund Hillary and Tenzing Norgay (them, themselves) can be humbled by the experience of climbing Mt. Everest.
4. The climb (itself, theirselves), not just reaching the top, proves your ability to conquer your fears.
5. You should never climb a mountain by (yourself, itself).

Name ______________________________ Date ______________

Reflexive and Intensive Pronouns *More Practice*

A. Identifying Reflexive and Intensive Pronouns

In each sentence, decide if the boldfaced pronoun is reflexive or intensive. Write **R** for reflexive or **I** for intensive on the line.

1. You **yourself** are your own best friend up in the mountains. ______
2. You can protect **yourself** from harm by taking a few important precautions. ______
3. Climbers risk exposing **themselves** to hypothermia and altitude sickness. ______
4. For that reason, wear protective clothes and remind **yourself** not to rush into high altitudes too quickly. ______
5. When we **ourselves** are careless, we put ourselves and others in danger. ______
6. Beware! An avalanche can propel **itself** to speeds of over 100 miles per hour. ______
7. To protect **yourself** against falling while ice climbing, you should place a screw in the ice every five to ten meters. ______
8. Even though he is a fine climber, Reinhold Messner **himself** takes the dangers of climbing seriously. ______
9. To prepare to climb, I enrolled **myself** in a rock climbing gym to experience climbing in a safe and controlled setting. ______
10. We **ourselves** determine whether we are successful climbers or not. ______

B. Choosing Reflexive and Intensive Pronouns

Fill in the blanks in the following sentences with appropriate reflexive or intensive pronouns. On the line to the right, write **R** for reflexive or **I** for intensive.

1. Let's give ______________ a fighting chance to win this game. ______
2. If left alone, the problem may just solve ______________. ______
3. I ______________ will testify if it will help your case. ______
4. Be careful you don't cut ______________ on that sharp blade. ______
5. It is we______________ who must speak out about the cheating. ______
6. Mr. Bacon ______________ told us that the pool was closed. ______

CHAPTER 3

Name ________________________________ Date ______________

Lesson 5

Reflexive and Intensive Pronouns

Application

A. Proofreading

Proofread the following page from a journal about a rock climbing experience. The writer wants to publish it in a magazine, but there are several reflexive and intensive pronoun errors. When you find a pronoun used incorrectly, cross it out. Then insert this proofreading symbol ^ and write the correct pronoun above it.

We had prepared us for months for the climb. Many of the team members theirselves practiced every day by bouldering. Whenever possible, we all practiced our moves on large boulders. However those boulders were only several feet off the ground. This was going to be different. Our trainer told us, "You must increase your strength, endurance, flexibility, and balance to succeed, but you also need to prepare you mentally for the climb." He was quite an experienced climber hisself. We always used ropes to protect us from falling. We used nuts, screws, and other tools to support us. Then the big day came. We started climbing a real cliff. It was difficult, but it was worth the effort. We congratulated us when we reached the top. We knew that we ourselves had what it took to be rock climbers.

B. Using Reflexive and Intensive Pronouns in Writing

What challenges have you overcome in your life? What lessons and skills have you learned in the process? Write a paragraph about a time when you faced a challenge and gained knowledge because of it. Use at least four reflexive or intensive pronouns in your paragraph.

CHAPTER 3

Name ______________________ Date ____________

Lesson 6

Interrogatives and Demonstratives

Teaching

An **interrogative pronoun** is used to introduce a question.

Interrogative Pronouns	Use
who, whom	refers to people
what	refers to things
which	refers to people or things
whose	indicates ownership or relationship

Who is always used as a subject or a predicate pronoun.

Subject Who was president during the Civil War?
Predicate pronoun The winner is who?

Whom is always used as an object.

Direct object Whom did you choose for your running mate?
Indirect object You told whom our secret?
Object of preposition For whom did the caller ask?

Don't confuse *whose* with *who's. Who's* is a contraction that means *who is.*

A **demonstrative pronoun** points out a person, place, thing, or idea. The demonstrative pronouns—*this, that, these,* and *those*—are used alone in a sentence. Never use *here* or *there* with a demonstrative pronoun.

Singular This is your last chance. That is the right answer.
Plural These are my favorite slippers. Those are too small.

A. Using Interrogative Pronouns

Underline the pronoun that correctly completes each sentence.

1. (Who, Whom) was the first man to walk on the moon?
2. To (who, whom) am I speaking?
3. (Who, Whom) did Abraham Lincoln choose as the general of the Union Army?
4. By (who, whom) was that song written?
5. (Who, Whom) will you invite to your birthday party?
6. (Who, Whom) went with Robert Peary to the North Pole?

B. Using Demonstrative Pronouns

Underline the correct pronoun to complete each sentence.

1. (That, Those) are the players with real talent.
2. (These, This) is one movie that could have been shortened.
3. (This here, This) is the row where our seats should be.
4. I'd have to say (that, that there) was a perfect cartwheel.
5. Did you know (that, those) was the first time I ever played that game?
6. I'm pretty good at card tricks. Let me try (these, these here).

CHAPTER 3

Name ________________________________ Date ____________

Lesson 6

Interrogatives and Demonstratives

More Practice

A. Using Interrogative Pronouns

In each sentence, underline the pronoun that completes each sentence correctly.

1. (Who, Whom) was the first to find a pass through these mountains?
2. (Who, Whom) did you ask to feed the cats while we are away?
3. Do you know (who, whom) the secretary of state is?
4. (Who, Whom) did the British elect as prime minister?
5. (Who, Whom) holds the world record in the pole vault?
6. For (who, whom) did you say you bought those earrings?
7. (Who, Whom) painted that big mural in the post office?
8. You gave (who, whom) your locker combination?
9. Your hero is (who, whom)?
10. By (who, whom) was the symphony composed?
11. (Who, Whom) did you just call on the phone?
12. With (who, whom) are you going to the dance?

CHAPTER 3

B. Choosing Demonstrative Pronouns

Fill in the blanks in the following sentences with appropriate demonstrative pronouns.

1. ________ is the building I was describing to you.
2. ________ are the recipes I got from my grandmother.
3. Look on the wall over the fireplace. ________ are pictures of my family.
4. Whenever ________ happens, I have to laugh.
5. If you gave me a choice, I would choose ________.
6. ________ are the moves that will make you a great player.
7. ________ is the reason why I keep an extra pair of shoes in my locker.
8. ________ are the mice I am training to go through the maze.
9. I know you want a CD player for your birthday, but ________ is too expensive.
10. Renee asked me to buy her some gloves, but ________ seem too small for her.
11. I'd like to join you on Sunday, but ________ is the day we visit my grandmother.
12. Your last dessert was good, but ________ tastes absolutely heavenly.

Name ______________________________ Date ______________

Lesson 6 Interrogatives and Demonstratives

Application

A. Writing Sentences with Interrogative and Demonstrative Pronouns

Write a sentence that you could use in the following situations. Follow the instructions in parentheses to write your sentence.

1. You want to know the name of the school principal. (Use *who.*)

____

2. You want to know who wrote a certain book. (Use *whom.*)

____

3. You want to know which team is playing your school team on Friday. (Use *who.*)

____

4. You want to know whom the principal chose to be hall monitor. (Use *whom.*)

____

5. You want to know to whom a letter should be sent. (Use *who* or *whom.*)

____

B. Using Pronouns in Writing

Imagine that you have moved to a new school. You would have many questions. Write five questions you would ask when you got to the school. Use interrogative pronouns both as subjects and as objects.

1. ______________________________

2. ______________________________

3. ______________________________

4. ______________________________

5. ______________________________

CHAPTER 3

Name ____________________ Date __________

Lesson 7

Pronoun Agreement

Teaching

The **antecedent** is the noun or pronoun that a pronoun refers to or replaces. Pronouns must agree with their antecedents in number, person, and gender.

Number Use a singular pronoun to refer to a singular antecedent. Use a plural pronoun to refer to a plural antecedent.

The sun warms the earth with its energy.

The stars sent out their light years ago.

Person The **person** (first person, second person, third person) of a pronoun must be the same as the person of the antecedent. Avoid switching from one person to another in the same sentence or paragraph.

First Person I enjoy watching stars through my telescope.

Second Person You can record your experiences in a journal.

Third Person Kari recognizes her favorite constellations.

CHAPTER 3

Gender The **gender** of a pronoun must be the same as the gender of its antecedent. Personal pronouns have three gender forms: masculine *(he, him, his)*, feminine *(she, her, hers)*, and neuter *(it, its)*. Do not use only masculine or feminine pronouns when you mean to refer to both genders.

Mr. Harcourt gets out his telescope on clear nights.

Mrs. Lopez remembers the stars over her childhood home.

An astronomer often records his or her observations.

Identifying Pronouns and Their Antecedents

In each sentence underline the personal pronoun once and its antecedent twice.

1. Take some time to look up at the stars. They are beautiful and fascinating.
2. Look at that constellation. Do you see that its stars, when connected, look like a hunter?
3. Some people can see a queen sitting on a throne when they look at a group of stars called Cassiopeia.
4. Gary says that he can't see how anyone could think these groups of stars look like queens or hunters.
5. Anna has studied the history of constellations, and she says that the ancient Greeks are the ones who named these groups of stars.
6. When the Greeks looked up, they told stories about the stars.
7. The arrangement of the stars reminded Greeks of characters in the stories they had told for years.
8. For example, the story connected to the constellation Cassiopeia tells of a vain queen. The gods chained her to a rock.
9. Orion, the great hunter, can be seen in the sky along with his faithful dog.

Name ______________________ Date ______________

Lesson 7

Pronoun Agreement

More Practice

A. Identifying Pronouns and Their Antecedents

In each sentence, draw an arrow to connect each pronoun with its antecedent.

1. Stargazing has kept its fascination for centuries.
2. Around 200 B.C., Babylonians looked up at the sky to find their future.
3. According to the Babylonians, the stars were important because their movements influenced events on Earth.
4. Today scientists believe human events are not influenced by the position of stars or their movements.
5. The sun, however, does affect life on Earth. It provides heat and warmth.

B. Making Pronouns and Antecedents Agree

On the line write a pronoun that correctly completes each sentence. Also underline the antecedent(s) of the pronoun.

1. Uncle Jack is driving a new pickup truck. He just bought ______________.
2. Marc should carry______________ own backpack.
3. Istanbul is a city in Turkey. ______________ former name was Constantinople.
4. Mandy brought her easel with ______________.
5. A good hiker will always bring ______________ first-aid supplies on a long hike.
6. Joyce and Traci go to the local gym because ______________ can swim in the pool there.
7. Blake and Steve put ______________ return bottles on the counter.
8. Mr. Lee moved ______________ lawn sprinkler several times.
9. You shouldn't forget ______________ umbrella today.
10. The players are already on the bus. ______________ have a game in Columbus today.

CHAPTER 3

Name ______________________________ Date ______________

Lesson 7

Pronoun Agreement

Application

A. Making Pronouns and Antecedents Agree in Writing

Read the following paragraph. Look especially for errors in agreement between pronouns and their antecedents. On the lines below, write the numbers of the sentences with agreement errors. Then write each of those sentences correctly. Use a separate piece of paper if necessary.

(1) Stars were Maria Mitchell's interest and their passion. **(2)** She was born in Nantucket, Massachusetts, in 1818. **(3)** When her father, who was interested in the stars, would study the sky on starry nights, he would join him. **(4)** Maria won fame in 1847, when it discovered a new comet. **(5)** In 1857, she went to Europe and had a chance to meet many famous astronomers. **(6)** Vassar College soon asked her to be her first professor of astronomy. **(7)** While Maria taught at Vassar, she refused to give your students grades because she didn't believe in them. **(8)** She asked students to trust yourself and observe the sky every night. **(9)** She studied sunspots and photographed it. **(10)** Maria Mitchell was an extraordinary astronomer in an era in which women were not encouraged in science.

CHAPTER 3

B. Writing with Pronouns

Have you ever spent time looking up at the sky on a clear night? What did you see there? Can you remember if you were alone or if someone else was with you? Write a description of such a night. Be sure to include at least four personal pronouns with clear antecedents.

Name ______________________________ Date ______________

Indefinite-Pronoun Agreement

Teaching

An **indefinite pronoun** does not refer to a specific person, place, thing, or idea. Indefinite pronouns often do not have antecedents.

Indefinite pronouns can be singular, plural, or singular or plural.

Indefinite Pronouns

Singular				Plural	Singular or Plural	
another	each	everything	one	both	all	none
anybody	either	neither	somebody	few	any	some
anyone	everybody	nobody	someone	many	most	
anything	everyone	no one	something	several		

Use a singular pronoun to refer to a singular indefinite pronoun. Use his or her when the antecedent could be either masculine or feminine.

Everyone brought his or her special dish to the picnic.

Use a plural personal pronoun to refer to a plural indefinite pronoun.

Several of the students brought their baseball mitts. (plural)

Some indefinite pronouns can be singular or plural. Often, the phrase that follows the indefinite pronoun tells you whether the indefinite pronoun is singular or plural.

All of the food was still in its basket. (*Food* is singular.)

All of the students made their own sandwiches. (*Students* is plural.)

Using Indefinite Pronouns

In each sentence, underline the correct pronoun. Also underline its antecedent.

EXAMPLE All of the teachers will have (his or her, their) pictures taken now.

1. All of the students in the class enjoyed (his or her, their) time away from school.
2. Everybody brought (his or her, their) backpack with dry socks and shoes.
3. None of the students wanted to miss (his or her, their) walk to the lake.
4. Neither of the teachers on the picnic wanted (their, his or her) students to go home with wet feet.
5. Some of the students said that they knew (his or her, their) way to the lake.
6. Both of the teachers were happy with (her, their) classes' behavior.
7. No one soaked (his or her, their) clothes in the lake.
8. Some of the lake pollution was down from (its, their) all-time high.
9. On the way back, everyone quickened (his or her, their) pace.
10. Each of the students wanted to save (his or her, their) place at the picnic tables.
11. Few in the group could resist (his or her, their) love for outdoor cooking.
12. Not surprisingly, all of the birds in the park wanted (its, their) fair share of the food too.

CHAPTER 3

Name ______________________________ Date ______________

Lesson 8

Indefinite-Pronoun Agreement

More Practice

A. Identifying Indefinite Pronouns

Underline the indefinite pronoun in each sentence. Then underline the correct pronoun in parentheses.

1. Before the math test, anyone can look at (his or her, their) book.
2. All of the girls were at (her, their) best in the last swim meet.
3. Both of the boys inherited (his, their) mother's red hair.
4. Sooner or later everyone must make (his or her, their) own decisions.
5. At the trial, each of the witnesses told (his or her, their) story.
6. Some of the students brought (his or her, their) own lunches.
7. Will anybody donate (his or her, their) time to the neighborhood cleanup?
8. Few in our class have reached (his or her, their) full height.
9. After lunch, everyone went (his or her, their) own way.
10. All of the speakers gave (his or her, their) talks in less than one hour.
11. Each of the cars had (its, their) headlights dimmed in the thick fog.
12. None of the perfume leaked out of (its, their) bottle.

CHAPTER 3

B. Using Pronouns Correctly

In each sentence below, decide whether the pronouns agree with their antecedents. If the sentence is correct, write **Correct** on the line. If it contains a pronoun that does not agree with its antecedent, rewrite the sentence correctly on the line.

1. Everybody was ready for their meal by about six o'clock.

____

2. Some of the boys were still playing their ball game.

____

3. Linda labeled each of the dishes with their name so everyone knew what it was.

____

____

4. Have any of the containers lost their lids?

____

5. Nobody wanted their feast to end.

____

Name ______________________________ Date ____________

Indefinite-Pronoun Agreement

Application

Lesson 8

A. Proofreading for Indefinite-Pronoun Agreement

Proofread the following paragraph. When you find a pronoun-antecedent error, cross the pronoun out. Then insert this proofreading symbol ⌃ and write the correct pronoun or pronouns above it. If necessary, mark any verb that must agree with the changed pronoun to be changed.

Everybody likes a picnic. But, when somebody planned the picnic I just came back from, they made a few mistakes. First, everybody brought their own dish to share, but everybody brought watermelon. There was watermelon everywhere. Luckily, many of the picnickers had also packed his or her cars with soft drinks and snacks. One of the members of one family had brought enough hamburger for her family, but not for everyone. So after a hearty meal of soft drinks, chips, and watermelon, many of the picnickers decided he or she would take a hike through the woods. Nobody had put any insect repellent in their backpacks, however, and the mosquitoes had the best picnic of all on the hikers' skin. When the hikers returned, they couldn't find any of the game equipment, so they had nothing to play with. Most of the people headed back to his or her cars at that point. Anyone who plans next year's picnic should make their preparations a little more carefully.

B. Using Indefinite Pronouns in Writing

Write a paragraph about a picnic you have attended. You may write about who was there and what you did and ate. Use at least four indefinite pronouns. Be sure that any personal pronouns agree with their indefinite-pronoun antecedents in number.

CHAPTER 3

Name ________________________________ Date ______________

Lesson 9

Pronoun Problems

Teaching

We and *Us* with Nouns

The pronouns *we* and *us* are often followed by a noun that identifies the pronoun *(we earthlings, us earthlings)*.

Use *we* when the noun is a subject or a predicate noun.

We earthlings saw the spaceship land. (We saw the space ship land.)

Use *us* when the noun is an object.

The aliens showed us earthlings the inside of their ship. (They showed it to us.)

Unclear Reference

Be sure that each personal pronoun refers clearly to only one person, place, or thing.

Confusing Courtney and Ann are best friends. She is upset that she is moving. (Who is upset? Who is moving?)

Clear Courtney and Ann are best friends. Courtney is upset that Ann is moving.

CHAPTER 3

A. Choosing the Correct Pronoun

In each sentence, underline the correct pronoun form.

1. (We, Us) fans waited outside the stadium.

2. When the coach saw (we, us) players, he asked us to carry the equipment bags.

3. (We, Us) customers waited in line for 15 minutes.

4. The bees stung (we, us) unlucky hikers.

5. The movie gave (we, us) inventors a good idea.

6. Once every summer, (us, we) neighbors get together for a block party.

7. To (we, us) couch potatoes, there's nothing like a Saturday afternoon movie.

8. When (we, us) contestants arrived, we were asked to sign in.

B. Avoiding Unclear Reference

In each set, circle the letter of the sentence that is stated more clearly.

1. a. Bill and Noah went to the lake, and he fell in.

b. Bill and Noah went to the lake, and Noah fell in.

2. a. When Mom and my sister went shopping, Mom couldn't decide what to buy.

b. When Mom and sister went shopping, she couldn't decide what to buy.

3. a. Before the Johnsons and Garcias met at the party, they didn't know they had just moved in down the street.

b. Before the Johnsons and Garcias met at the party, the Garcias didn't know the Johnsons had just moved in down the street.

Name ______________________________ Date ______________

Lesson 9

Pronoun Problems

More Practice

A. Choosing the Correct Pronoun

In each sentence, underline the correct pronoun form.

1. (We, us) earthbound creatures look up at the sky and ponder one question.
2. Are (we, us) humans the only thinking beings in the universe?
3. Getting to other galaxies seems impossible to (we, us) humans.
4. (We, Us) scientists don't believe anything that we can't prove.
5. To (we, us) doubters there is no possibility of travel at the speeds necessary to get beings from one galaxy to the other.
6. (We, Us) science-fiction writers are not bound by the facts.
7. Don't tell (we, us) dreamers that space travel between galaxies is not possible.
8. Maybe someone from outer space is trying to contact (we, us) believers right now.
9. To (we, us) futurists, the idea of space and time travel is fascinating.
10. No matter what scientists say, whenever (we, us) humans look out into space, we wonder.

B. Avoiding Unclear Reference

Rewrite each of these sentences to make them clear, not confusing.

1. Mom and Aunt Rita were talking on the phone but she could hardly hear her.

____

2. Both the planet and the star are clearly visible through the telescope, but I can't see it with the naked eye.

____

____

3. The brown horse and the white horse were running neck and neck, but suddenly it pulled ahead.

____

____

4. The Union soldiers and the Confederate soldiers battled for hours, but finally they started advancing.

____

____

5. I saw the movie and read the book, but I think I like it better.

____

6. Bob and Brian are going to the game. Today, he bought tickets for him.

____

CHAPTER 3

Name ______________________ Date ________

Lesson 9

Pronoun Problems

Application

A. Using Pronouns Correctly

Use each of the phrases printed below in an original sentence.

EXAMPLE we swimmers
We swimmers waited impatiently for the pool to open.

1. us fans ______________________

2. we mountain climbers ______________________

3. us winners ______________________

4. we readers ______________________

CHAPTER 3

B. Proofreading for Correct Pronoun Usage

The following paragraph is filled with unclear references. Rewrite the paragraph more clearly on the lines below.

Anita and Marisa were in class together yesterday, when suddenly she wasn't feeling well. She also felt sick. Their teacher sent them to the nurse's office. First she asked her what her symptoms were. She said that she had a headache and a stomachache. When she asked her, she said she felt about the same as Anita. She asked when she had started feeling sick. She decided that it was right about when she sat down in the classroom next to the chemistry lab. She called up to the classroom. Sure enough, a few more people were feeling sick now too. She called the principal and the teacher, and they had the students evacuate the hall near the chem lab. It's a good thing she had been there to put the clues together.

____

Name ________________________________ Date ______________

Lesson 10

More Pronoun Problems

Teaching

Using Pronouns in Compounds Use the subject pronouns *I, she, he, we* and *they* in a compound subject or a compound predicate pronoun. Use the object pronouns *me, her, him, us,* and *them* in a compound object.

Compound subject	Florence and he were daring people.
Compound predicate pronoun	Great adventurers were Samuel and she.
Compound object	Adventures were attractive to Samuel and her.

Phrases That Interfere Sometimes words and phrases come between a subject and a pronoun that refers to it. Be sure the pronoun agrees with the subject.

The Bakers, like other explorers, were determined to reach their goal.
(*Their* refers to *Bakers.*)

A. Using Pronouns in Compounds

Underline the pronoun that completes each sentence correctly.

1. Florence and Samuel Baker explored Africa; Florence and (he, him) were determined to find the source of the Nile River
2. Samuel and (her, she, he) set out on their journey in 1862.
3. For the first 1,000 miles, nothing but desert was visible to Samuel and (she, her).
4. Then a new problem confronted Florence and (he, him)—the swamp called the Sudd.
5. The group facing the challenge was Samuel, some helpers, and (her, she).
6. Mosquitoes attacked the couple and (them, they) as they slogged through the swamp.
7. Months later, Samuel and (she, her) became discouraged when they met someone who claimed to have already found the source of the Nile.
8. He told Florence and (he, him) that the source was Lake Victoria.
9. Florence and (he, him) weren't sure, so they continued their search.

B. Dealing with Phrases That Interfere

Draw arrows from the boldfaced pronouns to the words they modify.

1. The explorers who had been through so much still kept **their** determination.
2. After months, when the Bakers found Lake Albert, Samuel wrote in **his** journal that they had found the source of the Nile.
3. Even though he was later proven wrong, Samuel was recognized for **his** efforts, while Florence was ignored for **her** part in the exploration.

CHAPTER 3

Name ______________________ Date ______________

More Pronoun Problems

More Practice

A. Using Pronouns in Compounds

Underline the pronoun that completes each sentence correctly.

1. Billy and (she, her) went to the basketball game.
2. All the skiers followed Carolyn and (me, I) down the slope.
3. Between you and (I, me), this movie is not my favorite.
4. The most excited spectators were (we, us).
5. The dog trainer we admired the most was (she, her).
6. The audience had questions for Dr. Weiss and (he, him).
7. Dad gave Toshi and (he, him) a ride to the soccer game.
8. In Arizona, (she, her) and Carmen rode a dune buggy.
9. Mike and (I, me) stared at the hedgehog, and it stared back.
10. Janet made an ice sculpture for the twins and (we, us).

CHAPTER 3

B. Dealing with Phrases That Interfere

Decide if the pronouns in each sentence are used correctly. If the sentence has an error, rewrite it on the line. If the sentence is written correctly, write **Correct** on the line.

1. The Bakers, in spite of this setback, never lost sight of its goal.

   ____

2. Once, Samuel, trying to make a deal with a king in Africa, unknowingly agreed to exchange their wife for a guide.

   ____

   ____

3. Florence, although sick along the way, often rescued its husband from danger.

   ____

4. The canoe, while moving down the river, almost lost all its contents when a hippopotamus attacked.

   ____

   ____

5. The Bakers, desperate with hunger, sometimes ate crocodile meat as its supper.

   ____

   ____

6. Samuel, honored by a society of explorers, shared their reward with its wife.

   ____

Name ______________________________ Date ______________

Lesson 10

More Pronoun Problems

Application

A. Proofreading

Proofread this paragraph. Look especially for errors in the use of pronouns. When you find an error, cross out the pronoun used incorrectly. Insert this symbol ^ and write the correct pronoun above it.

Florence and Samuel Baker were not an ordinary couple. For one thing, European women in the 19th century were not known for their skill in canoeing down raging rivers, as Florence did. However, Samuel and her enjoyed the danger of exploration in Africa. To Samuel and she, the journey was serious business. Together, they planned a trip to find the source of the Nile River. Such a journey would be very dangerous. No one had done it before. In 1862, Samuel and she set out. On the way, they encountered many adventures. For example, the sight of a slave-trading center disgusted Florence and he. Civil wars slowed their progress. Samuel and her often became ill. Once, Florence lapsed into a coma, and Samuel thought that she would die. However, her and Samuel survived to become the first Europeans to stand at the shores of Lake Albert. Thanks to the efforts of Florence and he, the African continent became less mysterious to Europeans.

B. Making Pronouns Agree with Their Antecedents

Below are the beginnings of several sentences. Each beginning contains the sentence's subject. For each sentence beginning, write an ending that contains a pronoun that refers to the subject of each sentence.

EXAMPLE The cat with long whiskers licked *its fur*.

1. The explorers in Africa often lost ______________________.
2. The angry crocodile by the waterfall opened ______________________.
3. Florence, although sick, rose from ______________________.
4. Samuel, a good friend, was willing to share ______________________.
5. The assistants, each one weighted down with a heavy load, picked up ______________.
6. Africa, a mysterious continent to many 19th-century people, was known for __________

____.

CHAPTER 3

Name ______________________________ Date ______________

What Is a Verb?

Teaching

A **verb** is a word used to express an action, a condition, or a state of being. The two main kinds of verbs are action verbs and linking verbs. Both kinds can be appear with helping verbs.

An **action verb** tells what the subject does. The action may be physical or mental.

I **repair** cars. (physical action) I **know** a lot about cars. (mental action)

A **linking verb** links the subject of the sentence to a word in the predicate. The most common linking verbs are forms of the verb *be,* as in *We **are** late.*

Linking Verbs

Forms of *be*	be, is, am, are, was, were, been, being
Verbs that express condition	look, smell, feel, sound, taste, grow, appear, become, seem, remain

Some verbs may act either as action verbs or as linking verbs.

The chef **tastes** the desserts. (action)
The cake **tastes** delicious. (linking)

Helping verbs help the main verb express precise meaning. They are combined with the main verbs to form **verb phrases.**

He **has planted** the crops. (The helping verb is *has.* The main verb is *planted.*)

A few verbs can serve as either helping verbs or main verbs.

He **has** a tractor. (The main verb is *has.*)

Common Helping Verbs

Forms of *have:* has, have, had	Forms of *be:* be, am, is, are, was, were, been, being
Forms of *do:* do, does, did	Others: could, should, would, may, might, must, can, shall, will

Identifying Verbs

Underline the verb or verb phrase in each sentence. On the line to the right, label the verb with **A** for action or **L** for linking.

1. The technician programs the computers. ______

2. The marketer thinks of new marketing slogans for commercials. ______

3. An opera singer sounds amazing. ______

4. She was a banker, in charge of investment. ______

5. Every fireman smells for smoke at the scene of a fire. ______

CHAPTER 4

Name ______________________________ Date ______________

Lesson 1

What Is a Verb?

More Practice

A. Identifying Verbs

Underline the verb or verb phrase in each sentence. On the line to the right, label the verb with **A** for action or **L** for linking.

1. The teacher should take attendance every day. ______

2. The hard-working plumber was early. ______

3. Those secretaries appear very busy this afternoon. ______

4. A policeman did question the suspect after the incident. ______

5. The cab driver was driving extremely fast down the street. ______

6. Her mother, Naomi, is a tax attorney with her own business. ______

7. The construction crew will build that house in less than a month. ______

B. Identifying Helping Verbs and Main Verbs

In Exercise A, find four sentences that use helping verbs. In the chart below, write those sentence numbers and the parts of each verb phrase in the correct columns.

Number	Helping Verbs	Main Verb
______	______________	______________
______	______________	______________
______	______________	______________
______	______________	______________

CHAPTER 4

C. Using Verbs

In each sentence, replace the underlined verb. Use a more specific verb if possible.

1. My hairdresser <u>cleans</u> my hair before she cut it. ______

____

2. The reporter <u>makes</u> an article for the daily newspaper. ______

____

3. The florist <u>cuts</u> the ends of the flower stems. ______

____

Name ____________________ Date ____________

Lesson 1

What Is a Verb?

Application

A. Identifying and Replacing Verbs

In each sentence, underline the verb or verb phrase. If the verb is an action verb, rewrite the sentence with another action verb. If possible, use a more specific verb. If the original verb is a linking verb, simply write **Linking.**

1. The musician plays his guitar for the new band.

____

2. During the fall, we collect the leaves in our yard.

____

3. The veterinarian appears competent and friendly.

____

4. The painter did stir the paints together.

____

5. The coach knows the game of football very well.

____

6. The interior decorator recommended a new coat of paint.

____

CHAPTER 4

B. Using Verbs

On each line, write the action verb from the list below that makes sense in the sentence and paragraph. Be sure to use the correct form of the verb. Underline every linking verb.

to study **to tell** **to calculate** **to help** **to like**

Our class visited the Career Center today. It is interesting. The counselors ____________ us about the job opportunities available. For example, as a social worker, we could ____________ all the children who are less fortunate. Jennifer ____________ the ocean and its marine life. So, she might ____________ the ocean life as a marine biologist. For me, the job of an accountant seems appealing. I can ____________ answers to complicated math problems very easily. College degrees are necessary now for most professions.

Name ________________________________ Date ______________

Action Verbs and Objects

Teaching

Action verbs often require words that complete their meaning. These words are called **complements.** These complements are direct objects and indirect objects.

A **direct object** is a word or words that name the receiver of the action. It answers the question "What or whom receives the action of the verb?"

> Fred carries **letters**. (*What* does Fred carry? *letters*)

An **indirect object** tells to what or whom or for what or whom an action is done. Verbs that take indirect objects include *bring, give, hand, lend, make, send, show, teach, tell,* and *write.*

> Fred brings my **neighbors** mail. (*To whom* does Fred bring mail? *neighbors*)

(Note that if the preposition *to* or *for* appears before a word, that word is not an indirect object.)

Transitive and Intransitive Verbs An action verb that has a direct object is called a transitive verb. An action verb that does not have a direct object is an **intransitive verb.**

Do not be confused when an intransitive verb is followed by an adverb. A direct object tells *what* or *whom,* while an adverb tells *how, when, where,* or *to what extent.*

> Colby **reads** her mail. (*What* does Colby read? *mail.* Here ***reads*** is transitive.)
>
> Colby **reads** well. (*How* does Colby read? *well.* Here ***reads*** is intransitive.)

CHAPTER 4

Identifying Direct and Indirect Objects, and Transitive and Intransitive Verbs

In each sentence, underline the verb or verb phrase. Above each boldfaced word write **DO, IO,** or **ADV** for direct object, indirect object, or adverb. On the line to the right, write whether the verb is **Transitive** or **Intransitive.**

1. Henry forwarded **his lawyer** the **papers** by overnight mail. ______________
2. James practices **endlessly** at the gym. ______________
3. Uncle Leo mailed **James** a **basketball** for his birthday. ______________
4. James shipped **Uncle Leo** a **book.** ______________
5. Rhonda found the lost **stamps.** ______________
6. Janet didn't have an **envelope.** ______________
7. Mary **generously** gave **her** a large **envelope.** ______________
8. Frieda was scribbling **carelessly.** ______________
9. Frieda scribbled her **signature** on her cards. ______________
10. My mother sent **me** a care **package.** ______________

Name ______________________________ Date ____________

Lesson 2

Action Verbs and Objects

More Practice

A. Identifying Direct and Indirect Objects, and Transitive and Intransitive Verbs

In each sentence, underline the verb or verb phrase. Above each boldfaced word write **DO, IO**, or **ADV** for direct object, indirect object, or adverb. On the line at the right, write whether the verb is **Transitive** or **Intransitive.**

1. Morris dropped the **letter** at the post office.
2. On the address, the sender had written **illegibly.**
3. The librarian showed **Eva** a **letter** from the Second World War.
4. Malik sent **Nora** an **e-mail** with an explanation of his problem.
5. Dave submitted the winning **entry** in a contest.
6. He had received the entry **form** in the mail.
7. My mail **rarely** arrives on time.
8. Angela prepared beautiful **packages.**
9. The mail carrier handed **us** the **catalogs.**
10. **What** did your cousin send **you?**

B. Completing Transitive Verbs by Adding Direct Objects

Add a direct object to each of these sentences.

1. The mail carrier put ______________________ in the box.
2. Maria sent ______________________.
3. Dora mailed her brother ______________________.
4. Helen addressed ______________________ to the entrants.
5. Maria put ______________________ in a brown manila envelope.
6. The postal clerk gave Emilio ______________________ for his dollar.
7. Bart accepted John's ______________________ about the mix-up.
8. The applicant submitted ______________________.
9. A delivery truck brought us ______________________ on Friday.
10. As usual, the holidays caused ______________________ at the post office.

CHAPTER 4

Name ________________________________ Date ____________

Lesson 2

Action Verbs and Objects

Application

B. Changing Intransitive Verbs to Transitive Verbs by Adding Direct Objects

The verb in each sentence below is an intransitive verb, without a direct object. Rewrite the sentence, using the same subject and verb but changing the rest of the sentence to make the verb transitive. Underline both the verb and the direct object that you add.

EXAMPLE Mrs. Johnson dresses stylishly.
Mrs. Johnson dresses her little boy in warm clothes.

1. Christine writes well.

____

2. Thomas has sung a long time.

____

3. Hortensia knits skillfully.

____

4. The orchestra played out of tune.

____

5. My neighbor stopped for a chat before her trip.

____

CHAPTER 4

B. Using Direct and Indirect Objects and Transitive and Intransitive Verbs

Write a paragraph about sending mail (letters or packages) to a friend. In the paragraph, use at least four terms from each box. Use the verbs as either transitive or intransitive verbs. Use the nouns and pronouns as direct or indirect objects. Underline each verb you use as a transitive verb.

Verbs				Nouns and Pronouns			
made	stopped	brought	called	name	package	picture	girl
sent	told	showed	wrote	gift	note	story	boy
put	gave	taught	handed	her	him	us	them

____

____

____

____

____

Name ______________________ Date ______________

Linking Verbs and Predicate Words

Teaching

A linking verb connects the subject of a sentence to a word or words in the predicate. This word is called a **subject complement.** The subject complement identifies or describes the subject. Some common linking verbs are *is, feel, seem,* and *look.*

A hurricane **is** a violent tropical whirlwind. (linking verb: *is;* subject complement: *whirlwind*)

Hurricanes **seem** uncontrollable. (linking verb: seem; subject complement: *uncontrollable*)

There are two kinds of subject complements.

A **predicate noun** is a noun that follows a linking verb and identifies, renames, or defines the subject.

Some tropical storms **become** hurricanes. (The predicate noun *hurricanes* identifies the subject, *storms.*)

A **predicate adjective** is an adjective that follows a linking verb and describes or modifies the subject.

Their winds **are** strong. (The predicate adjective *strong* describes the subject, *winds.*)

CHAPTER 4

Identifying Linking Verbs and Predicate Words

In each sentence, underline the subject once and the verb twice. Write the predicate word on the line to the right.

1. A hurricane is a powerful tropical storm. ______________

2. For a hurricane, the water temperature must be warm. ______________

3. Feeder bands are the outer part of the hurricane. ______________

4. The eye is the center of the hurricane ______________

5. Inside the eye, the wind feels calm. ______________

6. Outside the eye, the winds grow fierce. ______________

7. That part of the hurricane is the eye wall. ______________

8. Hurricanes are dangerous over land. ______________

9. A surge is a quick rise in the ocean's water level. ______________

10. The winds of a hurricane sound deafening. ______________

Name ______________________________ Date ______________

Lesson 3

Linking Verbs and Predicate Words

More Practice

A. Identifying Linking Verbs and Predicate Words

In each sentence, underline the subject once and the verb twice. Write the predicate word on the line to the right.

1. Storm trackers are very important. ____________
2. These people seem unbelievably brave. ____________
3. Their hurricane targets are deadly. ____________
4. Temperature measurements are the goal of trackers. ____________
5. The information obtained appears essential to weather forecasters. ____________
6. Under the right conditions, any tropical storm can become a hurricane. ____________
7. Storm trackers are reliable information gatherers. ____________
8. Early evacuation warnings are necessary for safety. ____________
9. Andrew was a hurricane of 1992. ____________
10. Throughout Florida, its effects looked disastrous. ____________

CHAPTER 4

B. Using Predicate Words

Complete each sentence by writing a predicate complement in the blank. In the parentheses following the sentence, write **PN** if you added a predicate noun and **PA** if you added a predicate adjective.

1. To my grandmother, my favorite music sounds ______________. (____)
2. The weather outside my window looks ______________. (____)
3. China is a ______________ in the Eastern Hemisphere. (____)
4. With water and fertilizer, the plants grew ______________. (____)
5. That girl was the ______________ who finished first. (____)
6. The football team grew ______________ during practice in the August heat. (____)
7. The moon looks ______________ when it hangs low in the night sky. (____)
8. San Francisco was the ______________ that was hit by an earthquake in 1989. (____)
9. The sky seems ______________ after last night's storm. (____)
10. The air smelled ______________. (____)

Name ______________________ Date ____________

Lesson 3

Linking Verbs and Predicate Words

Application

A. Identifying Linking Verbs and Predicate Words

In each sentence, underline the subject once and the verb twice. Write the predicate word on the line to the right. After the predicate word, identify it by writing **PN** for predicate noun or **PA** for predicate adjective.

Example Today's weather forecast was an accurate prediction. *prediction, PN*

1. Snowstorms are a common occurrence in the North during January and February. ____________
2. Yesterday, our local high temperature was a record. ____________
3. The rain on the roof sounded pleasant. ____________
4. Summer days seem long. ____________
5. The thick fog looked solid. ____________
6. After the drought, the long rain was a welcome relief. ____________
7. By January 5, our snow was three feet deep. ____________
8. During the hot months, mosquitoes are a nuisance. ____________

B. Rewriting Predicate Phrases

Rewrite each predicate phrase in Exercise A. When possible, replace every predicate noun with a predicate adjective or replace the predicate adjective with a predicate noun.

Example Today's weather forecast was *a poor guess*. **or**
Today's weather forecast was *accurate*.

1. Snowstorms are ____________.
2. Yesterday, our local high temperature was ____________.
3. The rain on the roof sounded ____________.
4. Summer days seem ____________.
5. The thick fog looked ____________.
6. After the drought, the long rain was ____________.
7. By January 5, our snow was ____________.
8. During the hot months, mosquitoes are ____________.

Name ______________________________ Date ______________

Lesson 4

Principal Parts of Verbs

Teaching

Every verb has four basic forms called its **principal parts:** the present, the present participle, the past, and the past participle. With helping verbs, these four parts make all the tenses and forms of the verb.

I **admire** that singer. (Present)
I am **admiring** her high notes. (Present participle)
I **admired** her presentation. (Past)
I have **admired** her for years. (Past participle)

The Four Principal Parts of a Verb

Present	Present Participle	Past	Past Participle
admire	(is) admir**ing**	admir**ed**	(has) admir**ed**
listen	(is) listen**ing**	listen**ed**	(has) listen**ed**

There are two kinds of verbs: regular and irregular.

A **regular verb** is a verb whose past and past participle are formed by adding *-ed* or *-d* to the present. The present participle is formed by adding *-ing* to the present. Spelling changes are needed in some words, for example, *carr**y**–carr**ied**.*

Present	Present Participle	Past	Past Participle
listen	(is) listen + *-ing*	listen + *-ed*	(has) listen + *-ed*

Irregular verbs are discussed in the next lesson.

CHAPTER 4

Identifying Forms of Regular Verbs

Identify each underlined principal part of the verb. Write **Pres., Pres. Part., Past,** or **Past Part.** on the line to identify the present, present participle, past, or past participle form.

Example The orchestra has voted on the contract. *Past Part.*

1. Marian Anderson was called "a queen, a national treasure, an inspiration." ______________
2. She performed on Easter Sunday, 1939, at the Lincoln Memorial. ______________
3. The Daughters of the American Revolution had prevented her from singing at Constitution Hall. ______________
4. The DAR barred her from singing there because she was African American. ______________
5. Eleanor Roosevelt resigned from the DAR in protest. ______________
6. We still listen to Marian Anderson's recordings. ______________
7. My sister is planning to write a term paper about the incident. ______________
8. My father recalls hearing her sing "My Soul Is Anchored in the Lord." ______________

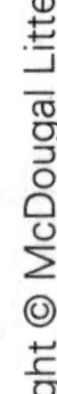

Name ______________________ Date ____________

Lesson 4

Principal Parts of Verbs

More Practice

A. Identifying Forms of Regular Verbs

Identify each underlined principal part of the verb. Write **Pres., Pres. Part., Past,** or **Past Part.** to identify the present, present participle, past, or past participle form.

1. Downtown, buses stop at every corner. ____________

2. Devora asked about any problems. ____________

3. Lonnie called me again just last week. ____________

4. The supervisor is threatening to reorganize the whole department. ____________

5. We are working on that problem now. ____________

6. After the fire, Jonathan offered his help. ____________

7. In a crisis, he always volunteers. ____________

8. Club officers had considered several alternatives to higher membership fees. ____________

9. Under other circumstances, Gloria would have contributed her time. ____________

10. The children are trying to help. ____________

CHAPTER 4

B. Writing the Correct Forms of Verbs

Decide which form of the verb given in parentheses is needed. Write the correct form on the line.

EXAMPLE The story has (remain) out in my memory. *remained*

1. The critics (acclaim) Miss Anderson's Town Hall concert in 1935. ____________

2. At age six, she was (perform) hymns with her church choir in Philadelphia. ____________

3. People over 70 years old (remember) her 1939 concert at the Lincoln Memorial. ____________

4. In 1943, she (perform) at Constitution Hall for a China Relief benefit. ____________

5. In 1942, for a second time, the DAR had (refuse) her permission to perform there. ____________

6. We are (look) through old newspaper files for her concert reviews. ____________

7. Sharon is (check) library files for her correspondence. ____________

8. I (wonder) if we will find any original letters. ____________

9. Her autobiography is (call) *My Lord, What a Morning.* ____________

10. We (consider) her a major figure in the struggle for dignity and equality. ____________

Name ______________________ Date ____________

Principal Parts of Verbs

Application

A. Writing the Correct Forms of Verbs

Decide which form of the verb given in parentheses is needed. Write the correct form on the line. Then identify which form you have used. Write **Pres., Pres. Part., Past,** or **Past Part** to identify the present, present participle, past, or past participle form.

EXAMPLE The horse has (jump) the fence. *jumped, Past Part.*

1. The police are (look) for clues. ____________
2. Ozzie has already (decide) on the color scheme. ____________
3. The men have (start) the engine in colder weather than this. ____________
4. Now the principal (doubt) Riva's story. ____________
5. Soon the new TV season will be (start). ____________
6. Yesterday, I (explain) our difficulty. ____________
7. Last night Mr. Vance (treat) us to dinner at the nicest restaurant in the city. ____________
8. Customers rarely (argue) about a billing error. ____________
9. The coach could have (complain) to the official. ____________
10. The team (play) every Friday night. ____________

B. Supplying Verbs in the Correct Forms

Almost all the verbs other than helping verbs are missing from this paragraph. On each blank line, write the verb from the list below that makes sense in the story. Be sure to use the correct form of the verb.

to encounter to face to acclaim to return to refuse to try

Marian Anderson ____________ racial prejudice and discrimination all her life. When, as a young girl, she ____________ to get into music school, she was ____________ admittance because of her color. She was 52 years old when she was permitted to sing at the Metropolitan Opera, though critics and concert audiences had been ____________ her performances for decades. She developed her career in Europe, where she ____________ less prejudice. When she ____________ to America, she sang a triumphal concert in Carnegie Hall.

CHAPTER 4

Name ______________________________ Date ____________

Lesson 5

Irregular Verbs

Teaching

Irregular verbs are verbs whose past and past participle are not formed by adding *-ed* or *-d* to the present. The five sections of this chart show different patterns used to form the past and past participles of many irregular verbs.

	Present	Past	Past Participle
Group 1 Forms of the present, the past, and the past participle are same.	cost hit hurt let put	cost hit hurt let put	(has) cost (has) hit (has) hurt (has) let (has) put
Group 2 The forms of the past and present participle are same	bring catch get leave sit	brought caught got left sat	(has) brought (has) caught (has) got (has) left (has) sat
Group 3 The past participle is formed by adding *-n* or *-en* to the past.	break choose freeze lie speak wear	broke chose froze lay spoke wore	(have) broken (have) chosen (have) frozen (have) lain (have) spoken (have) worn

	Present	Past	Past Participle
Group 4 The past participle is formed from the present, usually by adding *-n* or *-en*.	do eat fall give go know run see take throw	did ate fell gave went knew ran saw took threw	(has) done (has) eaten (has) fallen (has) given (has) gone (has) gone (has) run (has) seen (has) taken (has) thrown
Group 5 A vowel in the verb changes from *i* in the present to *a* in the past to *u* in the past participle.	begin drink ring sing swim	began drank rang sang swam	(has) begun (has) drunk (has) rung (has) sung (has) swum

The different forms of the verb *be* do not follow any pattern.

Present	Past	Past Participle
am, is, are	was, were	(have) been

CHAPTER 4

Using the Correct Forms of Irregular Verbs

Underline the correct verb form of the two in parentheses.

1. No one is sure when language (began, begun) in the human species.
2. Robert can (speak, spoken) Spanish as well as English.
3. Finally the driver (brought, brung) the huge truck to a halt.
4. The dog jumped up on the counter and (ate, eaten) half of the birthday cake.
5. Isaac Newton (did, done) major research in optics.
6. Have you ever (drank, drunk) goat's milk?
7. People dislike politicians who have (broke, broken) their promises.
8. The woman's smile (froze, frozen) upon her face.
9. Andre has (went, gone) swimming every day this summer.
10. Their hopes (fell, fallen) when the sailboat left without them.
11. I think you should have (gave, given) the server a larger tip.
12. Even in ancient times, some people (knew, known) that the earth is round.

Name ________________________________ Date ______________

Lesson 5

Irregular Verbs

More Practice

A. Using the Correct Forms of Irregular Verbs

Underline the correct verb form of the two in parentheses.

1. Late one night a scream (rang, rung) out in the dark courtyard.
2. Mark (grew, grown) a few inches last year.
3. We thought we (saw, seen) the light.
4. Kathryn (sang, sung) several Irish folk tunes at her recital.
5. Your friends (spoke, spoken) well of you when I saw them.
6. According to the accident report, the plane had (ran, run) out of gas.
7. Michelle has (stole, stolen) more bases than anybody else on our team.
8. She (took, taken) a chance in today's game, and it really paid off.
9. The catcher (threw, thrown) the ball to second base too late.
10. Until now, I had (wrote, written) off our team's chances of winning.
11. My little brother has (wore, worn) his favorite sweater every day this week.
12. This book (cost, costed) $8.99.

B. Writing the Correct Forms of Verbs

Decide which form is needed: the present participle, the past, or the past participle of each verb given in parentheses. Write the correct form on the line.

EXAMPLE Ms. Bronson has (teach) art for ten years. *taught*

1. Ernest Hemingway (choose) to live in Paris. ______________
2. Lisa (bring) cake to class on her birthday. ______________
3. Because spring was early, the fruit trees (begin) to bloom. ______________
4. The storm (break) several windows. ______________
5. When I had the flu, I (drink) a lot of fruit juice. ______________
6. Last winter (do) severe damage to the highways in this state. ______________
7. Rust had (eat) into the iron hull of the great ship. ______________
8. Clara (go) for the doctor in plenty of time. ______________
9. The police (give) the illegally parked car a ticket. ______________
10. The temperature (fall) last night. ______________

CHAPTER 4

Name ____________________ Date ____________

Lesson 5

Irregular Verbs

Application

A. Writing the Correct Forms of Verbs

Decide which form of the verb given in parentheses is needed. Write the correct form on the line. Then identify which form you used by writing **Past** or **PP** for past participle.

Example The sweater (shrink) when I washed it. *shrank, Past*

1. Our water pipes (freeze) during that cold snap last week. ____________
2. One of your ideas has really (ring) a bell with me. ____________
3. Regina (know) the answer to the question. ____________
4. My mother's family (grow) beans in Indiana before the Great Depression. ____________
5. I haven't (see) the northern lights since I lived in Canada. ____________
6. Woody Guthrie had (sing) his songs all over the country. ____________
7. I wanted to write you a letter yesterday, but I (run) out of time. ____________
8. When Sherri was in Kenya, she (speak) the Swahili language. ____________
9. Several planes have (take) off for the rescue mission. ____________
10. The fox (go) quietly into the chicken coop. ____________

CHAPTER 4

B. Proofreading for the Correct Forms of Verbs

Draw a line through each incorrect verb form in this paragraph. Draw this proofreading symbol ⌃ next to the error and, in the spaces between lines of type, write the correct form of the verb.

Example Jane ~~lended~~ ⌃ *lent* her doll to a friend.

My sister Jane is hard to please. For her birthday, I buyed her a sweater that I think she only weared once and then putted away in her closet. Last year, I got her a puzzle. A month later, without ever having put it together, she selled it at our annual garage sale for a dollar. I had payed $3 for it.

Name ______________________ Date ______________

Lesson 6

Simple Tenses

Teaching

A **tense** is a verb form that shows the time of an action or condition. Verbs have three **simple tenses:** the present, the past, and the future. The **present tense** shows an action or condition that occurs now. The **past tense** shows an action that was completed in the past. The **future tense** shows an action that will occur in the future.

Present Frieda **walks** quickly. She **is** quick.
Past Frieda **walked** quickly. She **was** quick.
Future Frieda **will walk** quickly. She **will be** quick.

The **progressive form** of a verb shows an action or condition that is in progress.

Present Progressive Frieda **is walking** quickly.
Past Progressive Frieda **was walking** quickly.
Future Progressive Frieda **will be walking** quickly.

The **present tense** is the present principal part of the verb. The **past tense** is the past principal part. To form the **future tense,** add will to the present principal part.

Tense	Singular	Plural
Present	I walk / you walk / he, she, it walks	we walk / you walk / they walk
Past	I walked / you walked / he, she, it walked	we walked / you walked / they walked
Future	I will walk / you will walk / he, she, it will walk	we will walk / you will walk / they will walk

To make the progressive form of one of these tenses, add the present, past, or future from of the verb *be* to the present participle of the verb, as in *I am walking, I was walking,* and *I will be walking.*

Recognizing the Simple Tenses

Identify the tense of each underlined verb. On the line, label the tense: **Present, Past, Future,** or **Present P., Past P.,** or **Future P.** for present, past, or future progressive.

1. The man next door is selling his car. ______________
2. From now on, he will use public transportation. ______________
3. Last year he was traveling to work on the bus once a week. ______________
4. This year he will be traveling by bus or walking every day. ______________
5. He plans to save some money by doing so. ______________
6. He figured up how much he will save. ______________
7. But best of all, he says, he will be saving the environment. ______________
8. He was feeling guilty about all the gasoline he used to get to and from work. ______________
9. Some of his co-workers are considering a similar move. ______________
10. My neighbor will encourage others to follow his example. ______________

CHAPTER 4

Name ____ Date ______________

Lesson 6

Simple Tenses

More Practice

A. Recognizing the Simple Tenses

Identify the tense of each underlined verb. On the line, label the tense: **Present, Past, Future,** or **Present P., Past P.,** or **Future P.** for present progressive, past progressive, or future progressive.

1. Are more people using public transportation these days? __________
2. The city is planning a campaign to encourage taking the subway. __________
3. Last year the rapid transit company purchased seven new railcars. __________
4. The city promotes use of the subway for fewer parking problems. __________
5. The common council will be conducting a survey on the whole issue. __________
6. How much do you figure the survey will cost? __________
7. Council members were considering a study on transportation earlier. __________
8. We decided buses and the subway are the easiest ways to get around. __________
9. Private transportation costs too much. __________
10. Public and private agencies are trying to change attitudes. __________

CHAPTER 4

B. Using the Simple Tenses

In each item, provide the requested form of the verb in parentheses.

1. (*work,* future progressive) The train operators __________________ on the holiday.
2. (*change,* present) The train schedule __________________ on the weekend.
3. (*arrive,* past) The noon train __________________ six minutes late.
4. (*update,* present progressive) Currently, the company __________________ the schedule.
5. (*revise,* past progressive) Managers __________________ it six months ago.
6. (*cause,* present progressive) The road reconstruction work __________________ a delay.
7. (*require,* past) That project __________________ the rerouting of traffic.
8. (*fund,* present progressive) The county __________________ 20 percent of the project.
9. (*cover,* future) State and federal grants __________________ the rest of the costs.
10. (*travel,* future progressive) I __________________ to school on different roads.

Name ______________________________ Date ______________

Simple Tenses

Application

A. Correcting Simple Tenses of Verbs

Although the times referred to in this paragraph vary from past to future, all of its verbs are in the present tense. Rewrite the paragraph, correcting verb tenses as needed. Use progressive tenses if the action is, was, or will be in progress. Underline every verb.

During the age of the horse and buggy, people complain forever about the smelly presence of horse manure in the streets. Then cars arrive on the scene. People proclaim the end of air pollution in the city. "From now on, we breathe clean air," they say. But they celebrate the new age of clean streets and clean air too soon. Today the auto fouls the atmosphere worse than ever.

____

____

____

____

____

B. Using Verb Forms Correctly

For each verb on the list, write the form requested in parentheses. Then write a paragraph about a topic of your choice that uses at least four of the phrases. Make sure all verb forms are used correctly.

(*like,* present) I ______________

(*walk,* past) I ______________

(*talk,* present progressive)
I ______________

(*hike,* future) I ______________

(*enjoy,* future progressive)
I ______________

(*observe,* past progressive)
I ______________

____

____

____

____

____

____

____

____

____

CHAPTER 4

Name ______________________________ Date ______________

Lesson 7

Perfect Tenses

Teaching

The **present perfect tense** shows an action or condition that began in the past and continues into the present.

Present Perfect Marty **has studied** math every day this semester.

The **past perfect tense** shows an action or condition in the past that came before another action or condition in the past.

Past Perfect Marty **had studied** her math before Ann called.

The **future perfect tense** shows an action or condition in the future that will occur before another action or condition in the future.

Future Perfect Marty will **have studied** her math before Ann calls again.

To form the **present perfect, past perfect,** and **future perfect tenses,** add *has, have, had,* or *will have* to the past participle.

Tense	Singular	Plural
Present Perfect *has* or *have* + past participle	I have studied you have studied he, she, it has studied	we have studied you have studied they have studied
Past Perfect *had* + past participle	I had studied you had studied he, she, it had studied	we had studied you had studied they had studied
Future Perfect *will* + *have* + past participle	I will have studied you will have studied he, she, it will have studied	we will have studied you will have studied they will have studied

CHAPTER 4

Recognizing the Perfect Tenses

Underline the verb in each sentence. On the blank, write the tense of the verb.

1. You have spoiled the dinner. ______________

2. Tom will have departed before Brian's arrival. ______________

3. Janet has refused any credit for the team's success. ______________

4. Many people had left before the fireworks. ______________

5. By this evening, I will have cleaned the whole downstairs. ______________

6. Before the end of our fight, we had avoided each other. ______________

7. The captains have examined all the team records. ______________

8. Prior to Tuesday, George hadn't suspected a thing. ______________

9. As judge, Thomas had decided on the winner before the end of the program. ______________

10. I will have learned all my verb forms by exam time. ______________

Name ______________________ Date ____________

Lesson 7

Perfect Tenses

More Practice

A. Recognizing the Perfect Tenses

Underline the verb in each sentence. On the blank, write the tense of the verb.

1. Jane had baked two cakes before the party. ____________

2. I have hiked these trails for 20 years. ____________

3. Olga had practiced on the piano up to the day of the contest. ____________

4. We will have covered ten miles by lunch time. ____________

5. He has hit more home runs than anyone else in the league. ____________

6. By next Saturday, Jenny will have logged 200 miles. ____________

7. At this rate, Dan will have scored 30 goals by the end of the season. ____________

8. The commander has talked about a different approach. ____________

B. Forming the Perfect Tenses

Complete each sentence by writing the form of the verb indicated in parentheses.

1. (*complete,* past perfect) We ____________ our assignment before the bell rang.

2. (*decide,* future perfect) Tory ____________ on an outfit by then.

3. (*realize,* past perfect) Joan ____________ her mistake before you told her.

4. (*work,* present perfect) Sue ____________ around the clock to finish on time.

5. (*select,* past perfect) The committee ____________ the winner already.

6. (*study,* future perfect) I ____________ two hours by the time she gets here.

7. (*hike,* present perfect) Matt ____________ the entire Appalachian Trail.

8. (*see,* future perfect) By the end of the year, Bill ____________ 40 movies.

9. (*bike,* past perfect) He ____________ 40 miles by the end of the day.

10. (*considered,* present perfect) The planners ____________ every angle.

CHAPTER 4

Name ______________________ Date ____________

Lesson 7

Perfect Tenses

Application

A. Using Verb Tenses

The following is a journal entry of a boy on a wilderness camping trip. Supply verbs to the narrative in the tenses indicated in parentheses. Choose verbs from the list below.

see surprise escape survive canoe

This trip has been a real adventure. We (present perfect) ______________ some amazing sights and have done some amazing things. Before we were in the woods half a day, we (past perfect) ______________ two small herds of deer grazing in clearings. So far we (present perfect) ______________ being eaten by a bear. We (present perfect) ______________ a day of white-water canoeing and plan to go again tomorrow. By the time we leave for home, I (future perfect) ______________ six rapids. I'm really enjoying this!

B. Using Verb Tenses

Choose a camping trip you have made or would like to make. Write sentences about the trip using the following verbs in the tenses indicated.

1. survive (future) ______________

2. carry (present perfect) ______________

3. canoe (past progressive) ______________

4. cook (future perfect) ______________

5. see (past perfect) ______________

6. discover (past progressive) ______________

7. enjoy (future perfect) ______________

8. learn (past perfect) ______________

CHAPTER 4

Name ______________________ Date ____________

Lesson 8

Using Verb Tenses

Teaching

In writing and speaking, you use the tenses of verbs to indicate when events happen. Changing tenses indicates a change in time. If you do not need to indicate a change in time between two actions, keep the tenses of the two verbs the same.

The Present Tenses These tenses show events occurring in the present time:

Present	Action occurs in the present.	watch, watches
Present perfect	Action began in past and continues in present.	has watched, have watched
Present progressive	Action is in progress now.	is watching, are watching

The Past Tenses These tenses show events that occurred in a past time:

Past	Action began and ended in the past.	watched
Past perfect	Action began and ended before another event in the past.	had watched
Past progressive	Action in the past was ongoing.	was watching

The Future Tenses These tenses show events occurring in a future time:

Future	Action will occur in the future.	will watch
Future perfect	Action will occur in the future before another action in the future.	will have watched
Future progressive	Action in the future will be ongoing.	will be watching

CHAPTER 4

Using Verb Tenses

Underline the verb form in parentheses that correctly completes each sentence.

1. When Mark Twain (was growing, is growing) up, the United States was smaller than today.
2. There (were, have been) few good roads at that time.
3. People of the time (prefer, preferred) to travel by boat than by horse or carriage.
4. Young Samuel Clemens (lived, will live) near the mighty Mississippi River.
5. He often (watched, watches) boats as they floated past.
6. No one (will be, had been) surprised to hear that the river looks different today.
7. When he (grows, grew) old enough, Sam Clemens got a job on a riverboat.
8. Soon he (learns, was learning) to pilot a riverboat.
9. Today we, too (learn, were learning) about riverboats through Twain's writing.
10. By the time he became a writer, Sam Clemens (will take, had taken) the name "Mark Twain" from a riverboat term.

Name ______________________________ Date ____________

Lesson 8

Using Verb Tenses

More Practice

A. Using Verb Tenses

Underline the verb form in parentheses that correctly completes each sentence.

1. In the early days of the United States, travel between the East Coast and the Midwest (was, is) difficult.

2. Even today, mountains (form, had formed) a barrier blocking westward travel.

3. Another barrier (has been, will be) the falls on the St. Lawrence River.

4. Merchants of the day (found, find) shipping goods westward impossible.

5. Around 1800, Canadians and U.S. citizens (look, were looking) for solutions.

6. In 1820, a private Canadian company (built, will build) a canal in Ontario.

7. For the first time, large boats (were, will be) able to travel past Niagara Falls.

8. During the next 130 years, the Canadian and U.S. governments (are discussing, were discussing) a larger system of canals.

9. Finally, in 1954, they (are beginning, began) work on the St. Lawrence Seaway.

10. After work on the Seaway (finishes, had finished), huge freighters traveled to ports on the Great Lakes.

B. Correcting Sentence Order

The sentences of this story are out of order. Read the story. Use the verb tenses and context to determine the correct order. Then rewrite the story in paragraph form below, with the sentences in correct order.

This year we are going canoeing again.
We thought we would catch fish and eat them.
We didn't take much food along—just a frying pan and some butter.
Last year we went on a canoe trip in the Adirondack Mountains.
We will be packing more food this time.
A local man told us, "The fish don't bite in this weather."
But we didn't catch any fish to speak of.

CHAPTER 4

Name ______________________________ Date ______________

Lesson 8

Using Verb Tenses

Application

A. Correcting Verb Tenses

Each underlined verb is in an incorrect tense. Write a correct form of the verb on the line.

1. Over the ages, ship builders <u>are trying</u> many different designs. ______________
2. Rafts <u>had been</u> simple and easy to build, but slow moving. ______________
3. When the Romans were conquering the world, private citizens <u>will travel</u> in cargo ships. ______________
4. Before Roman days, the Greeks <u>build</u> ships called *triremes.* ______________
5. A trireme <u>has</u> three decks of rowers to power the ship. ______________
6. Crew members on today's ships should be happy that none of them <u>had been asked</u> to row their ships. ______________
7. Some of the earliest boats we <u>had known</u> about were dugouts. ______________
8. By 2500 B.C., sailors of the Mideast <u>will be traveling</u> across the Mediterranean Sea. ______________

B. Correcting Sentence Order

Some of the verbs in this paragraph are in the wrong tense. Decide which verbs must be changed. Write the numbers of these sentences below. Then rewrite those sentences, correcting those verbs. Underline the verbs you have changed.

(1) Last year for my birthday, my parents took me to New York City. **(2)** We visit the Empire State Building and take a boat to the Statue of Liberty and Ellis Island. **(3)** I will like best the boat ride through the harbor to the statue and Ellis Island. **(4)** It made me think of the boat ride my great-grandfather took to come to Ellis Island as an immigrant. **(5)** My father says he still remembers his grandfather telling him the story of the ocean voyage. **(6)** When Great-grandfather arrives in New York, he sees the statue. **(7)** I am sure that I had always remembered that story too.

____

____

____

____

____

____

____

CHAPTER 4

Name ____________________ Date __________

Lesson 9

Troublesome Verb Pairs

Teaching

Do not confuse these pairs of verbs. Read how they differ, and study the chart.

lie/lay *Lie* means "to rest or recline." It does not take an object.
Lay means "to put or place something." It does take an object

set/sit *Sit* means "to be in a seat" or "to rest." It does not take an object.
Set means "to put or place something." It does take an object.

rise/raise *Rise* means "to move upward" or "to get up." It does not take an object.
Raise means "to lift (something) up." It usually takes an object.

may/can Use *may* when you are asking permission or if something is possible.
Can means "able to do something." *Can* and *may* do not have principal parts. They are used only as helping verbs.

May we help you? We can carry your packages.

	Present	Past	Past Participle
Lie* and *Lay	**lie** Rover lies at my feet.	**lay** Rover lay here earlier.	**lain** Rover has lain there.
	lay Ted lays a cup here.	**laid** He laid a cup there.	**laid** He has laid two cups.
Sit* and *Set	**sit** The cat sits there.	**sat** The cat sat there.	**sat** The cat has sat there.
	set She sets the box down.	**set** She set it down before.	**set** She has set it down.
Rise* and *Raise	**rise** We rise at 8 A.M.	**rose** We rose early.	**risen** You have risen early.
	raise Lee raises her hand.	**raised** Lee raised it.	**raised** Lee has raised it.

Using Troublesome Verbs Correctly

Underline the correct verb in parentheses.

1. Immigrant workers (lay, laid) the railroad tracks that crossed the United States.

2. As we speak, curious treasures (lie, lay) hidden at the bottom of the seas.

3. The old clock has (sat, set) on that ledge for a long time.

4. We'll have to (sit, set) a limit on spending next year.

5. It looks like it (can, may) rain this afternoon.

6. I (can, may) just barely see the playing field from here.

7. My grandparents (raise, rise) corn and beans on their farm.

8. Be sure to (raise, rise) when the mayor enters the room

9. When the old man had been (lain, laid) to rest, the mourners left.

10. (Sit, Set) the photograph up on the shelf where we can all see it.

Name ____ Date ______________

Lesson 9

Troublesome Verb Pairs

More Practice

A. Using Troublesome Verbs Correctly

Underline the correct verb in parentheses.

1. The sun (raised, rose) at 6:56 this morning.
2. Mary (raised, rose) her hand and waited patiently to ask a question.
3. Arnold (lay, laid) around yesterday.
4. He has (lain, laid) around all week.
5. Your boots are (sitting, setting) there, exactly where you left them.
6. Why don't you (sit, set) down your load and rest awhile?
7. (May, Can) I please have a cookie?
8. I think I (may, can) answer your question.
9. The bricklayer has (lain, laid) an amazing number of bricks today.
10. The wallet had (lain, laid) there unnoticed for nearly an hour.

B. Correcting Troublesome Verbs

Examine the boldfaced verb in each of the following sentences. If the verb is not correct, write the proper verb on the line. If the verb is correct, write **Correct.**

1. I've **set** here for an hour waiting for you. ______________
2. We'll need to **set** up more chairs on the lawn. ______________
3. A lovely old pearl **laid** at the bottom of the drawer. ______________
4. Let us **set** all our presents on the table. ______________
5. Mrs. Smith has **raised** three healthy boys. ______________
6. A small green shoot **raised** from the well-tended flower bed. ______________
7. **Can** I join your team? ______________
8. You **can** put those boxes on the truck if you are strong enough. ______________
9. The council member has **risen** an interesting question. ______________
10. When the trainer gives the signal, the dog will **lay** down on the grass. ______________

Name ______________________________ Date ______________

Lesson 9

Troublesome Verb Pairs

Application

A. Correcting Troublesome Verbs

Examine the boldfaced verb in each of the following sentences. If the verb is not correct, write the proper verb on the line. If the verb is correct, write **Correct.**

1. There the army **set,** waiting for reinforcements. ______

2. Those old magazines have **set** on the table for months. ______

3. We **lay** some keepsakes in the old strongbox. ______

4. The dogs **laid** in the sun all day. ______

5. We hope the old hen will **lay** an egg today. ______

6. I **rose** my grades this report card. ______

7. Questions about his innocence **rose** in my mind. ______

8. At least 15 birds were **sitting** on the wire. ______

9. From the tower, you **can** see all the way to the mountains. ______

10. Can I borrow a pencil? ______

CHAPTER 4

B. Using Troublesome Verbs Correctly

The following sentences contain five incorrectly used verbs. Rewrite the paragraph below, correcting all five errors

Being a house cat isn't easy. Some people think we just lay on windowsills all day. Others say we set on sofas and shed. But I get up before the sun raises and go to bed long after it sets. In between I have to pounce and stretch, scratch sofas, and keep an eye on my human. At the end of the day, as long as I may keep my eyes open, I patrol the house before I lay down for the night.

____

____

____

____

____

____

____

____

Name ________________________________ Date ____________

Lesson 1

What Is an Adjective?

Teaching

An **adjective** is a word that modifies, or describes, a noun or a pronoun.

Adjectives	
What kind?	slow train, slow car
Which one or ones?	last chance, second door
How many or how much?	three rows, several passengers

The most commonly used adjectives are the articles *a, an,* and *the.* *A* and *an* are **indefinite articles.** They refer to someone or something in general. Use *a* before a word beginning with a consonant and *an* before a word beginning with a vowel.

A train ride can be an enjoyable experience.

The is the **definite article.** It points out one specific person, place, thing, or idea.

The train arrives in ten minutes.

Many adjectives are formed from common nouns, such as *windy* from *wind.* **Proper adjectives** are formed from proper nouns. Proper adjectives are always capitalized.

Proper Nouns	Proper Adjectives
America	American
Canada	Canadian

Identifying Adjectives

Underline all the adjectives in each sentence.

1. The Fosters had a good time when they took a train to Chicago.
2. The excited family climbed aboard the train.
3. They found adjoining seats in an empty row.
4. Brad waited for the other passengers to board.
5. Finally, the train pulled out, and the dark train yard disappeared from view.
6. First, they saw the crowded city they were leaving.
7. But soon, the large city disappeared, and they could see the green countryside.
8. Cindy wondered if there was a Pullman car on the train, where tired people could sleep.
9. Mom and Dad got out the delicious lunches they had packed the night before.
10. Then they looked at the American countryside as they sped over the miles.
11. The long trip passed by quickly, and soon they were seeing the tall buildings of Chicago.
12. That was one trip the family will never forget.

CHAPTER 5

Name ______________________________ Date ______________

Lesson 1

What Is an Adjective?

More Practice

A. Identifying Adjectives and the Words They Modify

Underline each adjective once and the word it modifies twice. Circle the proper adjectives. Ignore the articles.

1. Sculptures have been made from many materials.
2. The first sculptors used bone and ivory.
3. Greek sculptors carved huge blocks of marble into human forms.
4. The ancient Greeks also made bronze statues.
5. African masks have been sculpted from wood.
6. At Mount Rushmore, a magnificent sculpture of four faces of presidents has been cut into a craggy mountain.
7. One artist piled rocks in a lake and called the arrangement a modern masterpiece.
8. A French chef in New York chisels ice sculptures.
9. Machine parts are used to form mechanical sculptures.
10. Neon lights have been used to create artworks.

B. Writing Adjectives

Write an adjective to complete each sentence.

Example On the *crowded* train, it was hard to find a seat.

1. On a ________________ trip, I like to take a good book to read.
2. At the beginning of a long train trip, I sat down in a ________________ seat.
3. I looked out the window at ________________ scenery.
4. A ________________ toddler sat in the row ahead of me.
5. Her ________________ mother tried to keep the child interested in coloring.
6. But the ________________ girl was more interested in me.
7. She leaned over the seats and stared at me with ________________ eyes.
8. She asked me ________________ questions.
9. The ________________ train ride was filled with conversation.
10. With a ________________ companion, it didn't seem so long after all.

CHAPTER 5

Name ______________________ Date ______________

Lesson 1

What Is an Adjective?

Application

A. Writing Adjectives in Sentences

Use the word at the beginning of each item as an adjective in a sentence.

EXAMPLE graceful *The graceful swans landed in a quiet lake.*

1. mysterious ______________________
2. beautiful ______________________
3. thirteen ______________________
4. many ______________________
5. African ______________________
6. snowy ______________________
7. fast ______________________
8. breakable ______________________
9. frightening ______________________
10. Asian ______________________

B. Writing a Paragraph Using Adjectives

Imagine that you are taking a long, cross-country train ride. What do you see when you look out the window? How could you describe your fellow passengers? Write a short paragraph about your trip. Use at least five adjectives in your description. Underline the adjectives in your paragraph.

CHAPTER 5

Name ______________________ Date ______________

Lesson 2

Predicate Adjectives

Teaching

A **predicate adjective** is an adjective that follows a linking verb and describes the verb's subject. The linking verb connects the predicate adjective with the subject.

Fire in the city is dangerous. (The linking verbs is *is*. The predicate adjective is *dangerous*.)

Often, forms of *be* are linking verbs, as in the above example. However, predicate adjectives can also follow other linking verbs such as *taste, smell, feel, look, become,* and *seem.*

Such a disaster seemed impossible. (The linking verbs is *seemed*. The predicate adjective is *impossible*.)

Identifying Predicate Adjectives

Underline the predicate adjective in each sentence. If the sentence has no predicate adjective, write **None** on the line to the right.

1. In 1871, the city of Chicago was already huge. ______
2. Over 350,000 residents felt proud of their beautiful city. ______
3. Most of the buildings in the city were wooden. ______
4. The hundreds of miles of sidewalk were wooden too. ______
5. But the beautiful city became deadly on the evening of October 8. ______
6. On that night, someone was careless. ______
7. How the fire started is still mysterious. ______
8. Soon, however, whole city blocks were burning. ______
9. The waterworks soon caught fire; without water, the firefighters were helpless. ______
10. The fire burned for more than a full day. ______
11. The blaze had caused about $200,000 in damages. ______
12. After the fire, about 100,000 people were homeless. ______
13. More people had lost everything they owned. ______
14. The people of Chicago were courageous. ______
15. The new Chicago they built was even better than the old one. ______

CHAPTER 5

Name ______________________ Date ____________

Lesson 2

Predicate Adjectives

More Practice

A. Identifying Predicate Adjectives and the Words They Modify

Underline the predicate adjective in each of the following sentences. Write the word it modifies on the line to the right.

1. The forest appeared silver in the moonlight. ____________

2. I felt uncomfortable on the first day of school. ____________

3. As we approach, the volcano seems gigantic. ____________

4. The woods smell fresh in springtime. ____________

5. The voice on the phone sounded quite strange. ____________

6. The weather has turned cold this week. ____________

7. Some timbers of the old barn have become weathered. ____________

8. In this rain, the path seems even longer than usual. ____________

9. Isn't this room cozy? ____________

10. What smells so delicious? ____________

B. Writing Predicate Adjectives

Complete each sentence with a predicate adjective. Write the predicate adjective on the line.

1. The Great Chicago fire must have been ____________.

2. People felt ____________ when they saw the flames near their homes.

3. The fire department was ____________ trying to get to all the calls.

4. The flames were extremely ____________.

5. The air smelled ____________.

6. After the fire, people felt ____________ with whoever had started it.

7. It was ____________ to see all the burned-out buildings.

8. Who could have been ____________ enough to set a whole city on fire?

9. The damage caused by the fire was ____________.

10. Luckily, owing to a great deal of effort, Chicago's recovery was ____________.

Name ______________________ Date ____________

Lesson 2

Predicate Adjectives

Application

A. Writing Predicate Adjectives in Sentences

Use the word at the beginning of each item as a predicate adjective in a sentence.

EXAMPLE creative *Artists are creative.*

1. careful ______________________
2. fancy ______________________
3. old ______________________
4. cheerful ______________________
5. gloomy ______________________
6. unexpected ______________________
7. great ______________________
8. full ______________________
9. crowded ______________________
10. ripe ______________________

B. Writing a Paragraph Using Predicate Adjectives

Suppose you had been in Chicago in 1871 when the Great Fire broke out. What might you have seen? How would you have felt? Write a short paragraph about your imagined experiences. Use at least four predicate adjectives in your description. Use a verb other than a form of *be* in at least two of the sentences. Underline the predicate adjectives in your paragraph.

Name ______________________________ Date ______________

Lesson 3

Other Words Used as Adjectives

Teaching

Some nouns and pronouns may work as adjectives. In other words, they may modify, or describe, nouns.

Pronouns as Adjectives

This, that, these, and *those* are **demonstrative pronouns** that can be used as adjectives. *My, our, your, his, her, its* and *their* are **possessive pronouns** that can be used as adjectives. **Indefinite pronouns** such as *all, each, both, few, most,* and *some* can be used as adjectives.

Demonstrative pronoun	These statues are lifelike.
Possessive pronoun	The emperor is guarded by his soldiers.
Indefinite pronoun	Many stories were told about the strange army.

Nouns as Adjectives

Some nouns function as adjectives.

Noun	The tomb was filled with jade jewelry.

Identifying Nouns and Pronouns Used as Adjectives

Underline the nouns or pronouns that are used as adjectives in each sentence.

1. In ancient China, the powerful emperor Qin Shi Huangdi ordered that a clay army be made for him.
2. These soldiers would stand guard over his tomb.
3. Each soldier has a fierce expression on his face.
4. People have only recently found this incredible treasure.
5. In 1974, some peasants were digging a well.
6. Imagine their surprise when they uncovered many old statues.
7. The clay these 10,000 soldiers are made from is called terra cotta.
8. Also buried with the emperor was a terra cotta chariot.
9. This war chariot is life sized and impressive.
10. In case the emperor needed his possessions in the afterlife, he made sure some silk clothes were buried with him.
11. His subjects also buried gold necklaces and jade jewelry for him to use.
12. The soldiers were arranged in battle formation, ready to defend their emperor.
13. Real soldiers probably modeled for the faces of the clay figures.
14. This army is well armed; each soldier has a weapon—either a bow, a sword, a spear, or a crossbow.
15. If you were as rich and powerful as Qin Shi Huangdi, maybe you would make your tomb as grand as this one.

Name ______________________________ Date ______________

Lesson 3

Other Words Used as Adjectives

More Practice

A. Identifying Adjectives and the Words They Modify

Underline the pronouns or nouns used as adjectives in the following sentences. Draw an arrow from the adjective to the word it modifies.

1. As a child Bob played with his toy army for hours.

2. At our house, we post important messages on the refrigerator door.

3. Put your dirty towels in the clothes hamper.

4. When you canoe, do you prefer wood paddles or plastic ones?

5. Those children built a snow fort in their yard.

6. Christy wants to put her feet in every clear mountain stream that we come upon.

7. Your paper airplane flies farther than my plywood airplane does.

8. The archaeologists found many clay pots in the tomb.

9. That cherry pie is for your school sale.

10. Most days, these wool pants feel too itchy for me to wear.

B. Writing Pronouns and Nouns Used Adjectives

Complete each sentence with a noun or pronoun that is used as an adjective. Write the adjective on the line.

1. The ______________ statues are beautiful.

2. The king lived in a ______________ castle.

3. His people lived in ______________ huts.

4. He was an amazing ruler. Do you know ______________ name?

5. I would like to have discovered ______________ underground army.

6. ______________ statues were built centuries ago.

7. ______________ person who sees these statues is amazed by the artistry of their creators.

8. The ______________ jewelry buried with the emperor is very valuable.

9. If ______________ travels take you to China, you should visit this amazing place.

CHAPTER 5

Name ______________________ Date __________

Lesson 3

Other Words Used as Adjectives

Application

A. Writing Adjectives in Sentences

Use the word at the beginning of each item as an adjective in a sentence.

Example stone *A stone house will last for many years.*

1. this ______________________
2. grass ______________________
3. antique ______________________
4. car ______________________
5. every ______________________
6. silk ______________________
7. many ______________________
8. paper ______________________
9. metal ______________________
10. our ______________________

B. Writing a Paragraph Using Pronouns and Nouns as Adjectives

Use each of the following nouns and pronouns as adjectives to describe a visit to a museum with many ancient works of art. Write your paragraph on the lines below. Underline each of the listed words in your paragraph.

marble	their	that	every
stone	your	those	some

CHAPTER 5

Name ____________________ Date ____________

Lesson 4

What Is an Adverb?

Teaching

An adverb is a word that modifies a verb, an adjective, or another adverb.

Modifying a verb Denise always shops at the mall.

Modifying an adjective She is usually particular about what she buys.

Modifying an adverb She comes to the mall very early.

Adverbs answer the questions *how, when, where,* or *to what extent.* **Intensifiers** are adverbs that modify adjectives or other adverbs. They usually come directly before the word they modify. Intensifiers usually answer the question *To what extent?*

Adverbs	
How?	slowly, quickly, quietly
When?	today, rarely, annually
Where?	nearby, there, around
To what extent?	rather, quite, extremely

Many adverbs are formed by adding the suffix *-ly* to adjectives. Sometimes a base word's spelling changes whey *-ly* is added.

Adjective	strong	immediate	easy
Adverb	strongly	immediately	easily

Identifying Adverbs

Underline all the adverbs in each sentence. If there are no adverbs in a sentence, write **None** on the line to the right.

CHAPTER 5

1. There is a big sale at the mall today. ________
2. People who shop wisely can save a great deal of money. ________
3. Denise always goes to sales. ________
4. In the past, she has been very lucky with her buys. ________
5. She bought a rather expensive necklace very cheaply. ________
6. She feels happy when she finds a real deal. ________
7. For example, she bought a nearly new tent once at the outdoors store. ________
8. She will rather proudly show you the suitcase that she bought for next to nothing. ________
9. If you want to find a good deal, stay close to Denise. ________
10. She is amazingly skillful in both spending and saving money. ________

Name ______________________________ Date ____________

Lesson 4

What Is an Adverb?

More Practice

A. Identifying Adverbs and the Words They Modify

Underline the adverbs in the following sentences. Draw an arrow from each adverb to the word it modifies.

1. A load of salmon arrived on the docks yesterday.

2. The guard walked very cautiously into the building.

3. Our space probe landed softly on the moon today.

4. The lifeguard swam extremely fast.

5. Quickly, we gathered our gear.

6. The busy beaver gnawed quite furiously on the tree trunk.

7. I am well pleased with my new job.

8. That boy is rather talented; he'll go far if he works hard.

9. The plumbers finally finished repairing the pipes today.

10. Quite suddenly, the horse bolted across the field.

B. Writing Adverbs

Complete each sentence with an adverb. Write the adverb on the line.

1. The shopping mall was ____________ busy the day Sean went shopping there.

2. ____________ all the stores were filled with customers.

3. Sean ____________ shops with a friend.

4. They ____________ stop at the ice-cream store in the center of the mall.

5. Sean and his friend were ____________ surprised to see that the ice-cream store was gone.

6. In its place was a ____________ new store.

7. They stepped ____________, and a clerk asked if she could help them.

8. They looked ____________ and saw computer games on all the shelves.

9. As dedicated game players, the boys were ____________ pleased with this new store.

10. On the other hand, where can they get a ____________ good ice-cream cone now?

Name ______________________ Date ____________

Lesson 4

What Is an Adverb?

Application

A. Writing Adverbs in Sentences

Use the adverb at the beginning of each item in a sentence.

Example late *I came late for the movie.*

1. carefully ______
2. slowly ______
3. quickly ______
4. very ______
5. completely ______
6. easily ______
7. gracefully ______
8. outside ______
9. close ______
10. gently ______

B. Writing a Paragraph Using Adverbs

Choose four of the following adverbs to use in a story about a shopping trip. Write the story on the lines below. Underline each of these adverbs and any other adverbs that you use in your story.

eagerly	very	suspiciously	suddenly	always
carelessly	extremely	mostly	later	never

______

______

______

______

______

______

______

______

______

CHAPTER 5

Name ______________________________ Date ______________

Making Comparisons

Teaching

Adjectives and adverbs may be used to compare people or things. Special forms of these words are used to make comparisons.

Use the **comparative** form of an adjective or adverb when you compare a person or thing with one other person or thing. Use the **superlative** form of an adjective or adverb when you compare someone or something with more than one other thing.

Comparative Seattle is <u>cloudier</u> than Phoenix.
Superlative Seattle is the <u>cloudiest</u> city in the United States.

For most **one-syllable** modifiers, add *-er* to form the comparative *(small, smaller)* and *-est* to form the superlative *(old, oldest).*

You can also add *-er* and *-est* to some **two-syllable** adjectives. With others, and with two-syllable adverbs, use the words *more* and *most (more careful, most calmly).*

To form the comparative or superlative form of most modifiers with **three syllables,** use the words *more* and *most (more dangerous, most dangerous; more clumsily, most clumsily).*

Be sure to use only one sign of comparison at a time (*harder,* not *more harder*).

The comparative and superlative forms of some adjectives and adverbs are formed in irregular ways: *good, better, best; bad, worse, worst; well, better, best; much, more, most; little, less, least.*

Identifying Comparative and Superlative Modifiers

On the line, label the boldfaced modifier **C** for comparative, or **S** for superlative.

1. Which city has the **best** weather in the United States? ______
2. That all depends on the kind of weather that appeals to you **most.** ______
3. Some people are **happier** seeing sunny skies than they are seeing cloudy skies. ______
4. They feel **more energetic** when the skies are blue than when they are gray. ______
5. Some people think **more accurately** when they are not distracted by warm days. ______
6. Maybe you would move to the **warmest** city in the United States. ______
7. If you like to ski, you may like a cold climate **better.** ______
8. Definitely, the **worst** weather is a bad storm such as a tornado or a hurricane. ______
9. What is **most amazing** is that everybody has different likes and dislikes when it comes to weather. ______
10. There is no one **finest** city that everyone can agree on. ______

CHAPTER 5

Name ____________________ Date __________

Lesson 5

Making Comparisons

More Practice

A. Using Comparisons

Underline the correct form of comparison for each sentence.

1. This is the (rainier, rainiest) season of the year.
2. Usually, we get (more, most) rain in August than we do in October.
3. Unfortunately, this year has been the (drier, driest) year in a long time.
4. Farmers are suffering (most terribly, more terribly) than most other people.
5. Their crops are (shorter, shortest) than they usually are at this time of year.
6. Farmers depend (more completely, most completely) on the weather than the rest of us.
7. Even city dwellers would be (happier, happiest) if it would rain a little.
8. Their lawns are getting (browner, brownest) than they would like them to be.
9. The city pools are (busier, more busier) than they were last year.
10. The reservoir is at the (lower, lowest) level it's been in decades.

B. Using Modifiers in Comparisons

After each sentence, write either the comparative or the superlative form of the word in parentheses, depending on what the sentence calls for.

1. The batter hit the ball (hard) than I could. __________
2. Of all these sweaters, which one do you like (well)? __________
3. My cold is (bad) today than it was yesterday. __________
4. Of the two towels, this one feels (soft). __________
5. Tortoises usually move (slow) than hares. __________
6. Our team is the (good) of all the teams in the league. __________
7. Your shoes look (new) than mine. __________
8. Which member of the glee club can sing the (loud)? __________
9. This puppy is the (small) of the litter. __________
10. The archaeologist washed this artifact (carefully) than the last one. __________
11. Everybody seemed (silent) than usual. __________
12. Last, the (valuable) paintings in the show were offered for sale. __________

CHAPTER 5

Name ______________________________ Date ______________

Making Comparisons

Application

A. Proofreading

Proofread the following paragraph. Look especially for comparison errors in adjectives and adverbs. If a sentence contains an error, rewrite it correctly on the line with the same number. If it is correct, write **Correct** on the line.

What places in the United States hold weather records? **(1)** Let's start with the windier place of all, Mount Washington, New Hampshire. **(2)** Which of these cities has the rainiest August: Little Rock, Arkansas, or Baltimore, Maryland? **(3)** Little Rock does, by a long shot. **(4)** Which of these two cities deals most often with heavy snows, Boston, Massachusetts, or Rochester, New York? **(5)** Let's just say that snow shovels last longest in Boston than they do in Rochester. **(6)** Which city has the higher temperature in the United States in January? **(7)** No U.S. city is more warmer than Honolulu, Hawaii, in January.

1. ______________________________

2. ______________________________

3. ______________________________

4. ______________________________

5. ______________________________

6. ______________________________

7. ______________________________

B. Using Comparisons in Writing

Suppose you went to the South Pole with a group of scientists. You would be up against some of the most challenging weather conditions you can imagine. Write a journal entry from a particularly interesting day at the South Pole. You may talk about the weather or about the sights you are seeing. Choose four of the words in the list below, and use their comparative and/or superlative forms in a paragraph for your journal. Underline the words you use.

cold	hot	warmly	welcome	brightly
blustery	windy	fast	frightening	good
white	freezing	slowly	sunny	bad

____

____

____

____

____

CHAPTER 5

Name ______________________________ Date ______________

Adjective or Adverb?

Teaching

Some pairs of adjectives and adverbs are often a source of confusion and mistakes.

Good or *Well*

Good is always an adjective; it modifies a noun or pronoun. *Well* is usually an adverb; it modifies a verb, adverb, or adjective. *Well* is an adjective when it refers to your health.

Adjective Today is a good day for a ball game.
Does the pitcher feel well enough to play?
Adverb I can see well from these seats.

Real or *Really*

Real is always an adjective: it modifies a noun or pronoun. *Really* is always an adverb; it modifies a verb, adverb, or adjective.

Adjective Seeing the game is a real treat.
Adverb I feel really lucky.

Bad or *Badly*

Bad is always an adjective: it modifies a noun or pronoun. *Badly* is always an adverb; it modifies a verb, adverb, or adjective.

Adjective That was a bad call.
Adverb He pitched badly last inning.

Using the Correct Adjective or Adverb

Underline the correct modifier from those given in parentheses.

1. This seats are (good, well), aren't they?
2. There seems to be a (real, really) big crowd at this game.
3. Our team has been playing (good, well) so far this year.
4. We have been (real, really) fortunate that all the players have stayed healthy.
5. For example, this pitcher could have been injured (bad, badly) when the ball came back toward him.
6. I'm glad he raised his glove (real, really) quickly and caught the ball.
7. I think we may have a (good, well) chance at the division championship this year.
8. We may be (real, really) contenders for the pennant.
9. Here comes a (good, well) hitter up to the plate.
10. Wow! He hit that ball (good, well)!
11. He can hit a (real, really) long ball, can't he?
12. I'll bet it feels (good, well) to run around those bases.
13. I feel (bad, badly) that Luis couldn't join us because of a (bad, badly) case of summer flu.
14. Maybe when he feels (good, well) again, he'll see a game with us.

CHAPTER 5

Name ______________________ Date ______________

Adjective or Adverb?

More Practice

A. Using the Correct Modifier

Underline the correct word in parentheses in each sentence. Label each word you choose as **ADJ** for adjective or **ADV** for adverb.

1. Denise writes (good, well) enough to be published. ________
2. At the Japanese restaurant, the shrimp tempura tastes (good, well). ________
3. Rosa played the part of Lady Macbeth (real, really) well. ________
4. The driver who caused the accident feels very (bad, badly) about it. ________
5. Dolores did quite (good, well) on her final exams. ________
6. If Jason rides his bike that (bad, badly) all the time, he may hurt himself. ________
7. After a week the milk turned (bad, badly) in the refrigerator. ________
8. By now it must smell pretty (bad, badly). ________

B. Writing with Adjectives and Adverbs

Decide if adjectives and adverbs are used correctly in the following sentences. If you find an error, rewrite the sentence on the line. If the sentence is correct, write **Correct** on the line.

1. That player looks good at the plate, but can he field good, too?

____

2. Our team has a real need for a good catcher.

____

3. The centerfielder is doing real good now.

____

4. He is so good at judging where a real well-hit ball will land.

____

5. The pitcher really wants to hit the ball good and feels badly when he strikes out.

____

____

6. He should feel badly only when he serves up pitches that are real easy to hit.

____

____

CHAPTER 5

Name ____________________ Date ____________

Lesson 6

Adjective or Adverb?

Application

A. Writing Sentences Using Adjectives and Adverbs Correctly

Write sentences using the adjectives and adverbs given.

1. good (adjective) ____________________
2. well (adverb) ____________________
3. well (adjective) ____________________
4. bad ____________________
6. badly ____________________
7. real ____________________
8. really ____________________

B. Using Adjectives and Adverbs Correctly

Read the conversation below. It contains several errors in the use of *good, well, real, really, bad,* and *badly.* Underline any errors you find. Then rewrite the conversation correctly on the lines below or on a separate piece of paper.

"I feel real good today, don't you?" asked Gina. "It's been a long time since I've seen a real baseball game."

Gary replied, "I feel great, too. This is my first baseball game in a really long time. And how many times can you see a team that's playing this good? The only thing I feel badly about is that Sean couldn't be with us."

"I called his mother yesterday, and he is doing pretty good, I guess. Maybe his recovery will be real fast, and he'll be as good as new in a few weeks."

"There's the opening pitch. Their batter has a real bad reputation for annoying pitchers who are throwing good. Let's see if his performance is as bad as his reputation."

____

____

____

____

____

____

____

____

CHAPTER 5

Name ____________________ Date ____________

Avoiding Double Negatives *Teaching*

Lesson 7

A **negative word** is a word that implies that something does not exist or happen.

Common Negative Words

barely	never	none	nothing	can't
hardly	no	no one	nowhere	don't
neither	nobody	not	scarcely	hasn't

If two negative words are used where only one is needed, the result is a **double negative.** Avoid double negatives in your speaking and writing.

Nonstandard I haven't never tasted artichokes.
Standard I haven't ever tasted artichokes. ***OR*** I have never tasted artichokes.

A. Recognizing the Correct Use of Negatives

Circle the letter of the sentence from each pair that uses negatives correctly.

1. a. We didn't have no fresh milk in the house.
b. We didn't have any fresh milk in the house.

2. a. We didn't have any idea where the pasta was stored.
b. We didn't have no idea where the pasta was stored.

3. a. I can't hardly boil water without burning it.
b. I can hardly boil water without burning it.

4. a. No one knew anything about making any meals except sandwiches.
b. No one knew nothing about making any meals except sandwiches.

B. Avoiding Double Negatives

Underline the word in parentheses that correctly completes each sentence.

1. There wasn't (nothing, anything) ready for the evening meal when my brother and I came home yesterday.

2. My mom (hadn't, had) hardly walked in the door before we started asking what was for dinner.

3. Neither of us had (ever, never) done any cooking before.

4. Mom said, "You aren't (never, ever) going to learn to cook if you don't start sometime. How about now?"

5. "You can't find this recipe (anywhere, nowhere) in that cookbook," she said.

6. In scarcely (no, any) time, she had assembled the needed ingredients.

7. "No one (should, shouldn't) feel helpless in the kitchen," she said, as she told us what to do.

8. No one could have given us (no, any) better gift than that cooking lesson.

Name ______________________________ Date ______________

Avoiding Double Negatives

More Practice

A. Using the Correct Modifier

Underline the correct word in parentheses in each sentence.

1. Haven't you (never, ever) eaten rattlesnake tail?
2. It's a delicacy that hardly (anybody, nobody) I know has enjoyed lately.
3. But that dish isn't (anywhere, nowhere) near as strange as the foods some people eat.
4. I'll bet you haven't tried (neither, either) rats or skunks for dinner.
5. Most people wouldn't eat (no, any) insects, at least knowingly.
6. Don't be sure there aren't (any, no) insect parts in your food though; some are allowed in hot dogs.
7. I (can't, can) hardly imagine eating bird's nest soup, made from the saliva of little birds called swifts.
8. I haven't (never, ever) eaten fish for breakfast, as people in Japan do.
9. I don't care how hungry I am. Nobody (couldn't, could) make me eat beetles.

B. Avoiding Double Negatives

Rewrite each sentence to avoid double negatives.

1. We couldn't find nobody to care for our cat while we were on vacation.

   ____

2. Our dog doesn't eat no food unless someone keeps it company.

   ____

3. The driver couldn't scarcely see the road through the heavy rain.

   ____

4. I haven't seen neither of your neighbors today.

   ____

5. Why can't I never get past this level in the computer game?

   ____

6. The librarian can't find nothing about my topic in his reference books.

   ____

   ____

CHAPTER 5

Name ______________________ Date __________

Lesson 7

Avoiding Double Negatives

Application

A. Avoiding Double Negatives

Choose one of these words to complete each sentence below. Be sure to avoid double negatives. Cross out each word after you use it.

no	never	anyone	anybody	ever	neither
hardly	no one	barely	hasn't	anything	nothing

1. I heard the doorbell, but I can't see __________ at the door.
2. I haven't __________ been to that restaurant. Have you?
3. Nancy could __________ hear the caller's voice on the phone.
4. Mark has seen the movie twice, but I have __________ seen it.
5. If you don't have __________ nice to say, say nothing at all.
6. Hasn't __________ ever told you that you shouldn't talk with your mouth full?

B. Revising a Paragraph with Double Negatives

The following paragraph contains several double negatives. Read each sentence and decide if it has a double negative. If it does, rewrite it correctly on the corresponding line below. If it is correct, write **Correct** on the corresponding line.

(1) Eating hasn't never inspired me to be adventurous. **(2)** I would rather have a plain old pizza than almost any weird food. **(3)** However, I know I'm missing out on some exciting food experiences. **(4)** For example, I can't hardly think of eating the fish eyes that Native Americans in Alaska eat. **(5)** Nobody won't ever see me eating shark or jellyfish casserole. **(6)** Don't never expect me to eat a sheep's stomach. **(7)** (If you are ever in Scotland, you might see sheep's stomach on the menu as haggis. **(8)** And please don't let nobody slip some prickly pear cactus fruit into my salad! **(9)** I won't eat nothing strange, and that's final.

1. ______________________
2. ______________________
3. ______________________
4. ______________________
5. ______________________
6. ______________________
7. ______________________
8. ______________________
9. ______________________

CHAPTER 5

Name ______________________________ Date __________

Lesson 1

What Is a Preposition?

Teaching

A **preposition** is a word used to show a relationship between a noun or pronoun and some other word in the sentence. A preposition is always followed by an object, either a noun or a pronoun.

Some common prepositions are *about, across, behind, beneath, beside, between, by, during, for, from, in, like, of, on, over, to, under, until, with,* and *without.*

A **prepositional phrase** consists of a preposition, its object, and any modifiers of the object. The **object of the preposition** is the noun or pronoun following the preposition.

> Dogs help humans in many ways. (The preposition is *in,* the object of the preposition is *ways,* and the prepositional phrase is *in many ways.*)

Sometimes the same word can be used as a preposition or as an adverb. If there is no object, the word is an adverb.

> **Adverb** My dog jumped up.
> **Preposition** The cat climbed up the tree.

A. Finding Prepositions and Their Objects

Underline the preposition in each sentence. Underline the object or objects of the preposition twice.

1. Dogs have been trained to perform a wide variety of jobs.
2. Watchdogs protect their owners' homes from burglars.
3. Guide dogs help their owners across the street.
4. Police dogs can smell drugs in suitcases.
5. Hunting dogs lead hunters to wild game.
6. Dogs are good companions for older people who may be lonely.

B. Recognizing Prepositions and Adverbs

Decide whether the boldfaced word is a preposition or an adverb. Write **P** on the line if it is a preposition. Write **A** if it is an adverb.

1. **Over** our heads, great formations of geese were flying north. ______
2. As they flew **over,** we thought we could hear their wild cries. ______
3. Please ask the children to come **inside** because of the storm. ______
4. With all that lightning, they will be safer **inside** the house. ______
5. After years on the bench, the judge decided to step **down.** ______
6. Alice fell **down** the rabbit hole. ______

Name ______________________________ Date ______________

What Is a Preposition? *More Practice*

A. Identifying Prepositions and Their Objects

Underline each preposition once. Circle the object of the preposition. Sentences may have more than one prepositional phrase.

1. Above her head sat the Cheshire cat.
2. The train roared through the tunnel, blasting its horn.
3. On Tuesday my father's car was parked inside the garage.
4. Hundreds of people swarmed into the theater for the concert.
5. Jan showed the lizard to her teacher before class.
6. At noon the colonel strode across the courtyard toward the gate.
7. Without doubt, spitting in the subway is against the law.
8. Our class has been running behind schedule until now.
9. Some of the disagreements between us are beside the point.
10. In the evenings of August, the katydids sang in the trees.

B. Writing with Prepositional Phrases

Underline the prepositional phrase in each sentence. Then replace that phrase with a different prepositional phrase, and write your new sentence on the line. Be sure to use a different preposition and a new object of the preposition.

Example The dog with the leather collar is mine.
The dog behind the fence is mine.

1. I took my dog to obedience class.
____
2. My dog's problem is that it runs after squirrels.
____
3. The class was held in the school gym.
____
4. The instructor made us walk around the room together.
____
5. We practiced walking beside each other.
____
6. During class my dog seemed happy and calm.
____

CHAPTER 6

Name ______________________ Date ____________

Lesson 1

What Is a Preposition?

Application

A. Writing with Prepositional Phrases

Add one or more prepositional phrases to each simple sentence. Write your new sentence on the line.

1. The sheepdog ran.

2. It barked.

3. The sheep moved.

4. The dog saw a wolf staring.

5. The dog got up and ran.

B. Writing with Prepositional Phrases

Use three of these prepositional phrases in an original story. Write your story on the lines below.

in the barn	with a strange name	down the road
by the pump	for fun	after the stranger
after sunrise	over the fence	near the house

CHAPTER 6

Name ______________________________ Date ______________

Using Prepositional Phrases

Teaching

A **prepositional phrase** is always related to another word in a sentence. It modifies the word in the same way an adjective or adverb does.

An **adjective phrase** is a prepositional phrase that modifies a noun or a pronoun. It can tell which one, how many, or what kind.

The room <u>with many doors</u> was confusing. (The phrase *with many doors* modifies the noun *room*.)

An **adverb phrase** is a prepositional phrase that modifies a verb, an adjective, or another adverb. It usually tells *where, when, how, why, how many, how much,* or *how far.*

Modifying a verb I stepped <u>into a huge hall</u>. (The phrase *into a huge hall* modifies the verb *stepped*.)

Modifying an adjective It was awesome <u>in its beauty</u>. (The phrase *in its beauty* modifies the adjective *awesome*.)

Modifying an adverb The doorknob turned easily <u>for its age</u>. (The phrase *for its age* modifies the adverb *easily*.)

Placement of Prepositional Phrases Place the prepositional phrase close to the word it modifies, or else you may confuse your readers.

Confusing With an angry roar, the mouse ran from a lion.
Better The mouse ran from a lion with an angry roar.

Identifying Prepositional Phrases

Underline the prepositional phrase in each sentence. If it is an adjective phrase, write **ADJ** on the line at the right. If it is an adverb phrase, write **ADV.**

1. Last night I had a dream about a strange castle. ______
2. As I remember, I was walking down a long hall. ______
3. On either side were beautiful statues. ______
4. Suddenly, a little man with a long beard called my name. ______
5. He asked me to follow him through the wall. ______
6. The wall before me was solid and hard. ______
7. The man disappeared before my eyes. ______
8. I decided that his request was impossible and continued my walk toward a tiny door. ______
9. The door had a small lock with a tiny key. ______
10. After I opened the door, I stepped into a dark forest. ______

Name ______________________ Date __________

Lesson 2

Using Prepositional Phrases *More Practice*

A. Identifying Prepositional Phrases

In each sentence, underline the word modified by the boldfaced prepositional phrase. On the blank, write **ADJ** or **ADV** to identify what kind of prepositional phrase it is.

1. People always park on this street **during rush hour.** ______
2. During those long summer afternoons, we read books **about pirates.** ______
3. The family camped **beside the clear lake.** ______
4. I found an old photo of my great-grandmother **in the attic.** ______
5. I know little **about any flowers** except roses. ______
6. Rabbits live in burrows and under piles **of brush.** ______
7. Hovercraft have been used **for transportation** in a number of places. ______
8. Jim Gary makes sculptures **of dinosaurs** from old car parts. ______
9. No one but a fool would run **across the highway** in that traffic. ______
10. That field **of corn** will be gone within a year. ______

B. Placing Prepositional Phrases

Rewrite each sentence, changing the position of one or more prepositional phrases so that the sentence is no longer confusing.

Example We see images in our dreams from our subconscious mind.
In our dreams we see images from our subconscious mind.

1. Dreams to real experiences are related in our lives.

____

2. Of their dreams some people remember none.

____

3. Many people in color dream.

____

4. Fantasy is in most dreams combined with fact.

____

5. Activity produces dreams in the brain.

____

CHAPTER 6

Name ______________________ Date ______________

Using Prepositional Phrases

Application

A. Revising Sentences with Misplaced Prepositional Phrases

Rewrite each sentence, changing the position of one or more prepositional phrases so that the sentence is no longer confusing.

EXAMPLE By the artist, the painting in the hall was signed.
The painting in the hall was signed by the artist.

1. Timothy mailed the letter to his grandmother in the post office.

____

2. Regina told us about the great vacation she had at lunch.

____

3. The clock stopped by the water fountain at 3:30.

____

4. Amanda threw her mother from the train a kiss.

____

5. We took photographs of the sea on the pier.

____

B. Using Prepositional Phrases as Adjectives and Adverbs

Add a prepositional phrase to each sentence. The type of phrase to add is indicated in parentheses after the sentence.

1. The dream was exciting. (Add an adjective phrase.)

____

2. I was running. (Add an adverb phrase.)

____

3. Turtles were chasing me. (Add an adverb phrase.)

____

4. Suddenly, a talking horse appeared next to me. (Add an adjective phrase.)

____

5. The horse and I came to a stairway. (Add an adjective phrase.)

____

Name ______________________________ Date ______________

Lesson 3

Conjunctions

Teaching

A **conjunction** is a word used to join words or groups of words. Different kinds of conjunctions do different jobs.

Coordinating conjunctions connect words or groups of words used in the same way. The words joined may be used as subjects, objects, predicates, or any other kind of sentence parts. Some common coordinating conjunctions are *and, but, or, nor, for, so,* and *yet.* Use *and* to connect similar things or ideas. Use *but* to contrast things or ideas.

For the rich, life in ancient China was elegant and easy.
Rich people at that time lived well, but they didn't live as long as modern people.

Correlative conjunctions are pairs of conjunctions that connect words or groups of words used in the same way. Common correlative conjunctions are *both . . . and, either . . . or, neither . . . nor, not only . . . but also,* and *whether . . . or.*

Both servants and masters may have lived on the palace grounds.

Identifying Conjunctions

Underline all the conjunctions in the following sentences. Remember that there are two parts to a correlative conjunction.

1. Suppose you traveled back in time and landed in China around 100 B.C.
2. You would see houses made of wood and painted with lacquer.
3. Some houses have two stories and are topped with a watchtower to use as a lookout for spotting enemies.
4. The people are at peace right now, but who knows what the future holds?
5. The rich people live close to others, yet they live in a grander style.
6. For example, they wear fine silk shoes, socks, and robes.
7. Their palaces are filled with paintings and bronze ornaments.
8. Their palace grounds contain not only gardens but also ponds.
9. If you visited, you would want to go into a palace, for you would find it lovely.
10. When people got sick at that time, they were given medicines such as cinnamon and ground magnolia bark.
11. Neither wealth nor power keeps anyone from dying, however.
12. When rich people died, their tombs were filled with beautiful and costly possessions.
13. The dead could not use these items, but they were buried with them anyway.
14. For example, a tomb might hold a woman's cosmetics and her clothes.
15. Some rich people were buried with either a real servant or with a clay servant.
16. The customs may seem strange, but most people were happy with the way they lived.

Name ______________________ Date __________

Lesson 3

Conjunctions

More Practice

A. Identifying Conjunctions

In the following sentences, underline the conjunctions.

1. Suppose you traveled in time back to Rome in 20 B.C., and you came to the house of a senator.
2. The house is on a busy street, but it is quiet and peaceful inside.
3. Many of the rooms front on an atrium, an open area that is used for relaxing and greeting visitors.
4. It is long ago, yet the house has a central heating system.
5. Rooms are decorated with either paintings or statues.
6. Not only rich people but also their servants live in the large house.
7. The floors are made of marble, and they are beautiful and strong.
8. The senator and his sons are well educated.
9. Usually, boys, but not girls, are tutored or attend school.
10. The senator's family has a lifestyle that is elegant but normal for its place, time, and position.

B. Using Conjunctions

Complete each of the following sentences with a coordinating conjunction or a correlative conjunction.

Example The job was hard, ____but____ it was also rewarding.

1. Lewis __________ Clark explored the West, __________ their story is fascinating.
2. I've never met Ms. Phelps __________ Mr. Olson, but I've heard about them.
3. We looked for a bus or a cab, __________ we ended up walking home.
4. I would like a sandwich __________ a glass of milk for lunch.
5. __________ children __________ adults enjoy the circus.
6. __________ you have the wrong phone number __________ you misdialed.
7. If __________ you __________ your brother wants to come, just let us know.
8. Deeane turned the light on __________ she could see where she was walking.
9. __________ we go __________ stay is up to you.
10. The speakers are small, __________ they have a big sound.

CHAPTER 6

Name ______________________________ Date ______________

Lesson 3

Conjunctions

Application

A. Proofreading

Proofread the following paragraph, adding appropriate conjunctions where they are needed.

Pioneer life in America during the 18th century was rough ______________ simple. The log cabins pioneers built weren't particularly pretty, ______________ they did the job of keeping people warm and dry. When the members of a pioneer family first reached their land, their first job was planting the garden ______________ they would have something to eat when winter came. Their next job was to build a house. Many families got together to put up a house, ______________ that get-together was called a *house-raising*. The men would cut the logs ______________ lift them into place. ______________ the men ______________ the women and children helped build the house. After the walls were up, they pushed clay, moss, ______________ mud between the logs. ______________ the family would be warm and dry ______________ uncomfortable during the winter depended upon how well each person did his ______________ her job. The finished cabin had ______________ floor ______________ windows, but it was better than living in a tent.

B. Writing with Conjunctions

On the lines below, write a description of your home for someone who has never seen it. In your description, use at least two different coordinating conjunctions and two correlative conjunctions. Write the conjunctions on the correct lines below.

____

____

____

____

____

____

Coordinating Conjunctions	**Correlative Conjunctions**
______________	______________
______________	______________

CHAPTER 6

Name ______________________________ Date ______________

Interjections

Teaching

An **interjection** is a word or short phrase used to express emotion, such as *wow* or *my goodness*.

<u>Oh</u>, I'm so hungry!
<u>Wow</u>! That bee is huge!

Identifying Interjections

Read each sentence. If it contains an interjection, write the interjection on the line at the right. If it does not contain an interjection, write **None** on the line.

1. Hooray! Summer vacation is finally here! ______________
2. Honestly, I thought the year would never end. ______________
3. Let's plan a huge picnic. ______________
4. Yum! I love picnic food! ______________
5. Gee, I wonder if it will rain on Saturday? ______________
6. Well, let's plan the picnic for that day anyway. ______________
7. Today is a simply wonderful day for a picnic. ______________
8. Awesome! Someone brought enough brownies for everyone. ______________
9. Ridiculous! Of course we can have dessert first today. ______________
10. Yuck! Who dropped the watermelon? ______________
11. Ow! What just stung me? ______________
12. Heavens! Was that a baseball whizzing past my ear? ______________
13. No, I can't eat another bite. ______________
14. Brrr! The water in the lake is still too cold for swimming. ______________
15. Who wants to play a game of touch football? Not me. ______________
16. Okay, who took the last soda? ______________
17. The rain is starting! ______________
18. Whew! We got everything packed away just in time! ______________

CHAPTER 6

Name ______________________ Date __________

Lesson 4

Interjections

More Practice

A. Identifying Interjections

Read each sentence. If it contains an interjection, write the interjection on the line at the right. If it does not contain an interjection, write **None** on the line.

1. Oh, my! It's been snowing all night, and our street is blocked! __________
2. Hooray! They've called off school today. __________
3. Let's make snow angels in the back yard. __________
4. Well, I would like some cocoa and a cookie now. __________
5. You found a good book to read? Excellent! __________
6. The cable on the TV is out! Nuts! __________
7. Frankly, I think snow days are terrific! __________
8. I wonder if our teacher feels the same way. __________
9. Ridiculous! What would she do without us? __________
10. Wow! That day went by too quickly! __________

B. Using Interjections

Write an interjection before each of these sentences.

EXAMPLE ___*Ouch!*___ I stepped on a tack!

1. __________, I would love to own that CD.
2. __________! That looks disgusting!
3. __________! We won!
4. __________! That makes no sense at all.
5. __________, I thought the last piece of pizza was mine!
6. __________! What is in this container in the refrigerator?
7. __________! It's so cold today!
8. __________, that song is one of my favorites.
9. __________! That is not what I mean.
10. __________! That's great news!

CHAPTER 6

Name ______________________________ Date ______________

Interjections

Application

A. Writing Sentences with Interjections

Write a sentence for each of these interjections. You can decide for yourself whether to use a comma or an exclamation point after the interjection. An exclamation point after an interjection shows stronger emotion than a comma does.

EXAMPLE ick *Ick! How long has that ice cream bar been here?*

1. ouch ______________________________

2. hello ______________________________

3. ugh ______________________________

4. whew ______________________________

5. yikes ______________________________

6. gee ______________________________

7. whoa ______________________________

8. well ______________________________

9. hey ______________________________

10. no ______________________________

B. Writing a Diary Entry with Interjections

Write a diary entry about a day when everything went wrong from the time you got up until the time you went to bed. You can write about a real day you experienced or about an imaginary one. Whenever you want to express emotion, use an interjection. Use at least four interjections.

CHAPTER 6

Name ______________________________ Date ______________

Lesson 1

Gerunds

Teaching

A **verbal** is a word that is formed from a verb but acts as a noun, an adjective, or an adverb.

A **gerund** is a verbal that ends in *-ing* and acts as a noun. A gerund phrase consists of the gerund with its modifiers and complements.

Allen enjoys singing more than acting.
He feels that singing well is impossible without lengthy training.

In sentences, gerunds and gerund phrases may be used anywhere nouns may be used.

As subject	Singing requires good breathing.
As predicate nominative	My favorite activity is singing.
As direct object	I love singing.
As object of a preposition	Rebecca takes lessons in singing.
As indirect object	I give singing my best effort.

A. Identifying Gerunds

In each sentence, underline every gerund.

1. Playing guitar well takes a great deal of skill.
2. Elena has a knack for composing ditties.
3. Francine likes performing for an audience but hates practicing.
4. Morgan isn't interested in playing in an orchestra.
5. Developing an ear for music takes time and careful listening.
6. Dale's goal is touring with a rock band.

B. Identifying Gerunds

Underline each gerund. On the blank, write how it is used: **S** for subject, **PN** for predicate nominative, **DO** for direct object, or **OP** for object of a preposition.

1. Eating just before his performance gave Ben a stomachache. ______
2. Jorge is anxious about learning music. ______
3. We encouraged his entering the competition. ______
4. Ron's problem was thinking he was the best player. ______
5. Once the season starts, skating is all Orville thinks about. ______
6. One of the hardest things in band is blending in with the other players. ______
7. Singing is the most fundamental form of music. ______
8. I appreciate your reading my composition. ______
9. Victor has a talent for finding words that fit the music. ______
10. Melanie's favorite pastime is listening to her little sister sing. ______

CHAPTER 7

Name ______________________________ Date ____________

Gerunds

More Practice

A. Identifying Gerunds

Underline each gerund. On the blank, write how it is used: **S** for subject, **PN** for predicate nominative, **DO** for direct object, or **OP** for object of a preposition.

1. Thomas likes listening to classical guitar. ______
2. He's interested in learning to play it, but needs a teacher. ______
3. His least favorite activity is playing scales. ______
4. While fixing the engine, the mechanic played a classical music station. ______
5. Winning is not the only reason to enter the contest. ______
6. Gina enjoys studying with a real artist. ______
7. Is practicing two hours a day enough? ______
8. Devonna's goal is entering a college with a highly rated music department. ______
9. In music and comedy, timing is everything. ______
10. The school solved the schedule conflicts by creating a new class. ______

B. Using Gerunds

Rewrite each sentence. Change the boldfaced word or words to a gerund. You may need to alter some other words in the sentence.

1. **To play** bluegrass has always been my goal.

____

2. I was afraid **to have** him as a teacher.

____

3. The difficulty is **to find** time to practice.

____

4. **To spend** time with friends is important.

____

5. He knows it is a sacrifice **to work** so hard.

____

Name ______________________ Date __________

Lesson 1

Gerunds

Application

A. Using Gerunds

Write sentences using the following gerunds in the sentence parts indicated.

1. shouting (subject) ______________________

2. telling (object of preposition) ______________________

3. singing (predicate nominative) ______________________

4. winning (direct object) ______________________

5. playing (your choice of function in the sentence) ______________________

B. Using Gerunds in Writing

You would like to get a summer job, but don't know what kind of work you are qualified for. In listing work experiences you have had, you recall these chores: you have taken care of your younger brother and sister; grocery shopped for your parents; mowed the lawn and trimmed hedges; prepared family meals of eggs or sandwiches; and vacuumed carpets. Write a statement, using five or more gerunds, that lists your experiences. You might conclude with a sentence suggesting jobs that these experiences prepare you for.

Name ______________________________ Date ______________

Participles

Teaching

A **participle** is a verb form that acts as an adjective. It modifies a noun or pronoun. There are two kinds of participle: **present participles** and **past participles.** The present participle always ends in *-ing.*

A cheering crowd distracts him. (The present participle *cheering* modifies *crowd.*)

The past participle of a regular verb ends in *-ed.* For irregular verbs such as *steal,* the past participle has a different ending.

Stunned, she didn't know what to say. (past participle of regular verb)
The stolen diamond was worth millions. (past participle of irregular verb)

Gerunds, participles, and verbs all end in *-ing.* Here is how you can tell the difference.

Word	Example	Tip
Gerund	The grasshopper enjoyed fiddling.	Could be replaced by a noun
Participle	The fiddling grasshopper did no work.	Could be replaced by an adjective
Verb	He was fiddling all summer.	Always used with a helping verb

A. Identifying Participles and Gerunds

Write **Participle** or **Gerund** to identify the boldfaced verbal in each sentence.

1. The **disappointed** crow went hungry that day. ______________
2. The **boasting** hare lost the race to the tortoise. ______________
3. **Removing** a bone from the wolf's throat was probably foolhardy. ______________
4. The grasshopper laughed at the **hardworking** ant. ______________
5. After barely **escaping** the cat, the country mouse returned to the farm. ______________
6. The **frightened** rabbits, in turn, frightened the frogs. ______________
7. **Arguing** with the wolf was stupid. ______________
8. The fox tried to escape by **running** into the woods. ______________
9. The **choking** wolf begged the crane for assistance. ______________
10. The crane didn't get the **promised** reward. ______________

B. Identifying the Role of Participles

Underline the word that each boldfaced participle modifies.

1. The characters in Aesop's fables are **talking** animals.
2. **Reported** to be a slave in classical Greek times, Aesop was a great storyteller.
3. **Presenting** moral lessons, Aesop's fables guide children to right actions.
4. The tales, **retold** for generations, still entertain us.
5. We laugh at, yet learn from, the animals **acting** like humans.

Name ______________________ Date ____________

Lesson 2

Participles

More Practice

A. Identifying Participles and Gerunds

Underline the verbal in each sentence. On the line, write **Participle** or **Gerund** to identify the verbal.

1. The smiling man in the third row is my uncle. ____________
2. The slave Aesop was a master at telling stories. ____________
3. Pleased by the noisy applause, the singer gave an encore. ____________
4. Have you heard our whistling teapot? ____________
5. Kathy said she saw a spotted owl. ____________
6. That nursery is famous for growing beautiful orchids. ____________
7. All the candidates praise working people. ____________
8. Evan bought all the materials for building a boat. ____________
9. Taking this roundabout path was a mistake. ____________
10. Shocked by the sight of her sister after many years, the old woman wept. ____________

B. Identifying Participles and Participial Phrases

Underline the participle or participial phrase in each sentence. On the blank to the right, write the word that the participle or participial phrase modifies.

1. The lying fox only wanted to eat the chickens. ____________
2. Stopping too often for naps, the hare lost his race with the tortoise. ____________
3. Frustrated, the fox said the grapes were probably sour anyway. ____________
4. The eagle, convinced by the crow, let go of the turtle. ____________
5. The lion lay in front of his cave, gasping for breath. ____________
6. The disappointed crane flew off sadder but wiser. ____________
7. Running to the pond, the rabbits scared the frogs. ____________
8. The fox, expecting a nice meal, arrived at the crane's home. ____________
9. Thoroughly upset by the cat, the country mouse quickly left the city. ____________
10. Quarreling among themselves, the oxen became easy prey to the lion. ____________

Name ______________________ Date ____________

Lesson 2

Participles

Application

A. Using Participles in Writing

Write a sentence using each of these phrases made up of noun plus a participle.

1. screeching brakes ______________________

2. stunning outfit ______________________

3. disappointed contestant ______________________

4. crying baby ______________________

B. Using Participles and Gerunds

In each sentence, underline the verbal. On the line to the right, write **Gerund** or **Participle** to identify the verbal. Then rewrite the sentence, if possible changing each gerund to a participle and each participle to a gerund. Add words and ideas as needed.

EXAMPLE Croaking kept the frogs next to the pond busy. *Gerund*
The croaking frogs sat next to the pond.

1. Playing his fiddle all day, the lazy grasshopper wasted the summer. ____________

2. My favorite after-school pastime is talking on the phone. ____________

3. A smiling fox can't be trusted. ____________

4. The whistling waiter left the room. ____________

5. Studying for a test is difficult. ____________

Name ______________________ Date __________

Infinitives

Teaching

An **infinitive** is a verb form that usually begins with the word *to* and acts as a noun, an adjective, or an adverb. In each example below, the infinitive is *to exercise.* An **infinitive phrase** consists of an infinitive plus its complements and modifiers. The entire phrase functions as a noun, adjective, or adverb.

As noun To exercise is essential for good health. (subject of sentence)
John plans to exercise daily. (direct object)
His plan is to exercise daily. (predicate noun)

As adjective A plan to exercise is necessary. (*to exercise* modifies *plan*)

As adverb To exercise regularly, John made a schedule. (*To exercise* modifies *made,* telling why he made a schedule.)

To decide whether a phrase is an infinitive or a prepositional phrase, look at the word after *to.* If the word is a verb, the phrase is an infinitive. If the word is a noun or pronoun, the phrase is a prepositional phrase.

John is going to the movies. (prepositional phrase)
Would you like to go to the movies? (infinitive phrase)

A. Identifying Infinitives

Underline the infinitive in each sentence.

1. Kenneth's goal is to win the race.
2. The committee decided to present a trophy to the winner.
3. Who wants to race on Saturday?
4. The runners wanted to show their appreciation.
5. To compete, you must be diligent in your training.
6. Ann wants to run all the hills.
7. After the second mile, the runners stopped to get water.
8. To be on the team, you must show up for every practice.
9. His desire to win is almost a sickness.
10. The team manager tried to stay with the runners.

B. Identifying the Role of Infinitives

Write how each boldfaced infinitive is used: **N** for noun, **ADJ** for adjective, or **ADV** for adverb.

1. **To play** basketball with grace is Michael's gift. ______
2. The team struggled **to make** the playoffs. ______
3. Their desire **to win** the city championship is admirable. ______
4. **To achieve** their goal, they must work harder. ______
5. The team's fans hope **to see** a victory. ______

Name ______________________ Date ____________

Lesson 3

Infinitives

More Practice

A. Identifying Infinitives

Underline the infinitive in each sentence. On the blank, write how it is used: **N** for noun, **ADJ** for adjective, or **ADV** for adverb.

1. To compete in the Olympics is the dream of most athletes. ______
2. To make the Olympics, you must be talented and diligent. ______
3. The desire to excel is what motivates athletes. ______
4. She wanted to return home with an Olympic medal. ______
5. His hope was to win a medal in the 100-meter dash. ______
6. He had reason to think he could do it. ______
7. To be in the Olympics is a great achievement. ______
8. Athletes from around the world went to compete. ______
9. I wish they hadn't decided to allow professionals into the Olympics. ______
10. The effect of the change was to take something from the games. ______

B. Using Infinitives

Use each of the following infinitives in a sentence.

1. to read

____

2. to compete

____

3. to sail

____

4. to speak

____

5. to pitch

____

CHAPTER 7

Name ______________________ Date ____________

Lesson 3

Infinitives

Application

A. Using Infinitive Phrases

Use each of the following infinitives or infinitive phrases in a sentence.

1. to struggle

____

2. to play second base

____

3. to be the star

____

4. to race

____

5. to hit a home run

____

B. Using Infinitive Phrases

Rewrite each sentence, substituting an infinitive or infinitive phrase for the underlined words.

EXAMPLE Glenn was eager for the experience of trying out for the team.
Glenn was eager to try out for the team.

1. For the purpose of winning the race, Iona trained morning and night.

____

2. Ned's desire was becoming the goalie on the hockey team.

____

3. Pam's hope of playing second base created conflict between us.

____

4. Failure was never acceptable to Stephen.

____

5. All the coach wanted was success for the team.

____

CHAPTER 7

Name ______________________ Date ______________

Lesson 4

Verbal Phrases

Teaching

A **verbal phrase** consists of a verbal and any modifiers or complements it may have.

A **gerund phrase** consists of a gerund plus its modifiers and complements. Like a gerund, the entire phrase is used as a noun.

Flying a kite can be fun. (*Kite* is the complement-object of *flying;* the gerund phrase *Flying a kite* is used as the subject of the sentence.)

There are also useful reasons for flying a kite. (used as object of preposition)

A **participial phrase** consists of a participle plus its modifiers and complements. The entire phrase modifies a noun or pronoun.

Flying a kite in a storm, Benjamin Franklin was almost hit by lightning. (The participial phrase *Flying a kite in a storm* modifies *Benjamin Franklin.*)

An **infinitive phrase** consists of an infinitive plus its modifiers and complements. The entire phrase functions as a noun, an adjective, or an adverb.

Ben decided to fly a kite in a storm to test his theory about lightning. (The first infinitive phrase is used as a noun, telling *what* Ben decided; the second is used as an adverb, telling *why.*)

Identifying Verbals and Verbal Phrases

Identify each boldfaced verbal phrase by writing **gerund phrase, participial phrase,** or **infinitive phrase** on the line to the right.

1. **Using the kite string as an electrical conductor,** Franklin captured a bit of lightning. ______________
2. The electricity **captured during his experiment** was safely stored in a Leyden jar. ______________
3. Franklin's **surviving the process** was a kind of scientific miracle. ______________
4. **Knowing how dangerous it was,** Franklin surely would never have attempted his kite experiment. ______________
5. I remember how my father loved **flying kites.** ______________
6. He loved **to get out** in the city park on a windy autumn afternoon. ______________
7. But he always warned me never **to fly a kite in a storm.** ______________
8. **Using balsa sticks and tissue paper,** he made me my first kite. ______________
9. I remember **thinking it was not very handsome.** ______________
10. I'd give anything **to have that kite now.** ______________
11. **Remembering my first kite** brings back a lot of other memories. ______________
12. **Remembering my first kite,** I'd like **to make a kite** for my son. ______________

Name ______________________ Date __________

Lesson 4

Verbal Phrases

More Practice

A. Identifying Verbals and Verbal Phrases

Underline every verbal and verbal phrase in these sentences. If a sentence has more than one verbal or verbal phrase, use double underlining on the second one.

1. Anybody devoted to personal fitness should try to walk more.
2. After running, I only wanted to take a nap.
3. A flying trapeze is not the best equipment to exercise on.
4. Sailing inspired Henry to write poetry.
5. My least favorite exercise is running.
6. To build up muscles for running, Ari walked a mile a day.
7. Injured in the fall, Evelyn considered dropping out of the race.
8. Larry, surrounded by guards, decided to toss the ball at the basket.
9. Tony wanted to start a career in acting.
10. When people try to sail around the world, what do they do about receiving mail?

B. Identifying Verbals and Verbal Phrases

Identify each boldfaced verbal phrase in two ways. First, write **GP, PP,** or **IP** for gerund phrase, participial phrase, or infinitive phrase. Second, write how the phrase is used: **NS, NO, ADJ,** or **ADV** (for Noun as Subject, Noun as Object of verb or preposition, Adjective, or Adverb).

1. **To do your best,** you must develop a positive attitude. __________
2. Abner wanted **to try out** for the basketball team. __________
3. **Watching you try out,** I decided I should too. __________
4. **To win** was not his objective. __________
5. **Running track** is what Jackie lives for. __________
6. **Inspired by Ronald's attitude,** we tried harder. __________
7. In the sixth inning, Val scored the run **tying the game.** __________
8. I prefer **sailing my boat** to work. __________
9. My brother always likes a peanut butter sandwich after **swimming.** __________
10. **Observing your performance,** I learned a lot. __________

CHAPTER 7

Name ______________________________ Date ____________

Verbal Phrases

Application

A. Using Verbals and Verbal Phrases

What do you know about kites? Write sentences about kites using the verbal phrases identified in parentheses. Underline your verbal phrase.

1. (gerund phrase) ______________________________

____

2. (participial phrase) ______________________________

____

3. (infinitive phrase) ______________________________

____

B. Using Verbals and Verbal Phrases

Complete each sentence with a verbal or verbal phrase. On the numbered lines below, identify the verbal you supplied in two ways. First, write **G, P,** or **I** for gerund, participle, or infinitive. Second, write how the verbal is used: **N, N, ADJ,** or **ADV** for noun, adjective, or adverb.

Have you ever flown a kite? **(1)** ____________ is not difficult. You need **(2)** ____________ a kite and string. The easiest way to launch a kite is **(3)** ____________ into the wind, **(4)** ____________ the kite aloft, until the wind lifts it into the sky. **(5)** ____________ by the wind, the kite will gain and lose altitude. Listen to the taut string **(6)** ____________ in the wind. You'll want **(7)** ____________ back often to the park **(8)** ____________ your kite.

1. ____________ **5.** ____________

2. ____________ **6.** ____________

3. ____________ **7.** ____________

4. ____________ **8.** ____________

Name ______________________________ Date ______________

Lesson 1

What Is a Clause?

Teaching

A **clause** is a group of words that contains both a subject and a verb. There are two kinds of clauses, independent and dependent.

An **independent clause** expresses a complete thought and can stand alone as a sentence. An independent clause is also called a **main clause.**

We all want bargains.
SUBJECT VERB

A **dependent clause** may contain a subject and a verb, but it does not express a complete thought. It cannot stand alone as a sentence. Another name for a dependent clause is a **subordinate clause.** Dependent clauses are often introduced by words such as *because, when, if, while,* or *that.*

when we buy things
SUBJECT VERB

A dependent clause can be joined to an independent clause to express a complete thought.

We all want bargains when we buy things.

Identifying Independent and Dependent Clauses

Identify each boldfaced group of words by writing **IND** for independent clause and **DEP** for dependent clause.

1. Anyone with a checking account keeps track of the checks **that he or she writes.** ______
2. **Your check register is a record of your checks and their amounts.** ______
3. Veronica, **who is a very organized person,** keeps good financial records. ______
4. If you don't keep track of your funds, **you might write a bad check.** ______
5. A bad check is called bad **because there is no money in your account to pay it.** ______
6. **An orderly register tells the exact amount of money in your account.** ______
7. **If you have little or no money left,** you cannot write any more checks. ______
8. A bank charges an extra fee **whenever your funds won't cover your checks.** ______
9. **Each month, the bank sends you a statement** that shows what came into or went out of the account. ______
10. Every bank has its own rules about **what fees it charges.** ______
11. A checking account **that has a certain amount of money in it** will earn interest. ______
12. Before Andrew opened his checking account, **he asked about the bank's fees.** ______

Name ______________________________ Date ______________

Lesson 1

What Is a Clause?

More Practice

A. Identifying Independent and Dependent Clauses

Identify each boldfaced group of words by writing **IND** for independent clause or **DEP** for dependent clause.

1. My favorite store went out of business **because it was losing money.** ______

2. The store made many sales, but the prices must have been too low. ______

3. Perhaps the problem was **that the expenses were simply too high.** ______

4. When the store paid its own bills, there was no money left. ______

5. Naturally, the people **who owned the store** weren't happy. ______

6. The owners announced that they were selling the store. ______

7. Although the store has been closed for six months, I still miss it. ______

8. I had hoped to work at that store when I was old enough for a job. ______

9. Doesn't the activity in a store appeal to you? ______

10. Maybe the mall **where the store was** charged a high rent. ______

11. If I ever start a store of my own, I'll watch costs carefully. ______

12. Before I open the store, **I'll learn more about running a store.** ______

B. Identifying and Correcting Fragments

This paragraph includes three dependent clauses that are not attached as they should be to independent clauses. Rewrite the paragraph, connecting the dependent clauses to independent clauses.

Most teenagers get an allowance. They can spend this money. However they choose. Some teens spend the money on clothing and other items that they need. Others spend their allowance carelessly on things. That are soon thrown away. Many teens save some of their allowance. Teens who save will have money. When they really need it.

____

____

____

____

____

____

Name ______________________ Date __________

Lesson 1

What Is a Clause?

Application

A. Identifying Independent and Dependent Clauses

If an item is a sentence consisting of only one independent clause, write **IND** on the line. If it is a fragment consisting of only a dependent clause, write **DEP.** If the item is a sentence consisting of both an independent and a dependent clause, write either **IND + DEP** or **DEP + IND** to show the order of clauses.

Example After the snow fell. *DEP*

1. Banks pay interest on the money that customers loan them. ______
2. Although savings accounts pay interest, the rate is usually low. ______
3. When customers take out loans, they pay the bank higher interest. ______
4. When my brother started college. ______
5. While opening a checking account has strict requirements, even children can open savings accounts. ______
6. Loretta has had a savings account since she was six years old. ______
7. Because 4th Street Savings and Loan pays high interest. ______
8. Some banks encourage savings accounts for young people. ______
9. Other banks charge fees on accounts that have only a few hundred dollars in them. ______
10. If you leave money in a savings account for at least six months. ______

B. Correcting Fragments

In Exercise A, which items were fragments with the answer DEP? Write the numbers of those items on the lines below. Then complete each item by adding an independent clause to the dependent clause. Write the corrected sentence after the item number.

Example After the snow fell.
EX. The roads were slippery after the snow fell.

Revision of # ___ ______________________________

____

Revision of # ___ ______________________________

____

Revision of # ___ ______________________________

____

Name ______________________ Date __________

Simple and Compound Sentences *Teaching*

A **simple sentence** has one independent clause and no dependent clauses. Even a simple sentence can be elaborate, and it may have compound parts.

The squirrel found and buried the nut. (compound verb)

A **compound sentence** has two or more independent clauses joined together, but no dependent clauses. The clauses must be close in thought. They may be joined by a coordinating conjunction (with a comma) or by a semicolon.

The squirrel climbed the bird feeder, **and** the birds flew away.
The squirrel climbed the bird feeder; the birds flew away.

The coordinating conjunctions are the following:

for and nor or but so yet

Identifying Kinds of Sentences

Identify each sentence below with **S** for simple or **CD** for compound.

1. Greg shoveled the snow, and his brother began a snow sculpture. ______
2. The boat nosed up to the dock; our trip was finally over. ______
3. Tom and Gail quickly cut and stacked the firewood. ______
4. Several people listened, but nobody volunteered. ______
5. Sheila calls it a dragonfly; I call it a darning needle. ______
6. Did you and Lee walk or ride to your dance class? ______
7. Gina and Dave picked the wildflowers, and we arranged them. ______
8. The clown made a face; the child burst into laughter. ______
9. Her mother went to the trade show, but Doreen stayed home. ______
10. Wang and his brother looked at the problem and spotted the solution. ______
11. Mrs. Ballak may be in court, or she may be in her office. ______
12. Snow fell; winter was now upon us. ______
13. Kathy phoned this morning, but our phone was out of order. ______
14. The radio crackled with static and then went out. ______
15. We could play a video game, or we could go to Jim's house. ______
16. Lou has been baking bread, and Connie is making a big salad. ______

Name ______________________________ Date ____________

Lesson 2

Simple and Compound Sentences

More Practice

A. Identifying Kinds of Sentences

Identify each sentence below with **S** for simple or **CD** for compound.

1. Everyone played pretty well, but Jenny scored the winning basket. ______
2. Jaime and Ana sorted the photos and then framed them. ______
3. Jaime did most of the work, but Ana helped. ______
4. Toshi went to the mall on Saturday; Jody stayed home. ______
5. The motorcycles roared around the curve and raced down the track. ______
6. Will you stay home, or will you come with us to the movies? ______
7. I wrote her several times, but I never received an answer. ______
8. Charlene clutched at the brake; the bike finally stopped. ______
9. Tony washed and dried the dishes and cups. ______
10. Lawyers argue cases, but judges decide them. ______

B. Combining Sentences

Combine the two sentences in each item to make a compound sentence. Use a semicolon alone, or a comma with one of the coordinating conjunctions: *and, but, or, nor, for, so, yet.*

1. Dennis plays sports a great deal. He studies hard too.

____

____

2. You can walk to school today. You can take the bus.

____

____

3. The whale shark is the largest of all fish. It does not attack people.

____

____

4. Margarita hurt her leg. She didn't complain.

____

____

Name ______________________ Date __________

Lesson 2

Simple and Compound Sentences

Application

Combining Sentences

In all but three of the following items, the two simple sentences can be combined into one compound sentence. If the sentences are close in thought, combine them, using a semicolon alone, or a comma with a coordinating conjunction: *and, but, or, nor, for, so, yet.* If the sentences are not close in thought, write **Unconnected Simple Sentences.**

1. The temperature rose above freezing. The snow finally began to melt.

____

____

2. Stanley turned on the bedroom light. His mother was making dinner in the kitchen.

____

____

3. Amy can play the guitar. She can play the piano.

____

4. The hare slept. The turtle ran.

____

5. Carlos bought a tie. He still needed a jacket.

____

6. Classes are canceled on Thursday and Friday for Thanksgiving. In Canada, Thanksgiving is celebrated during a different month.

____

____

7. Andrea likes soccer. Her brother prefers swimming.

____

8. Nita mailed the letter today. The post office was crowded.

____

9. Keith completed the test. He forgot to write his name on it.

____

____

Name ______________________ Date ____________

Lesson 3

Complex Sentences

Teaching

A **complex sentence** has one independent clause and one or more dependent clauses.

> **Fossils, as you may know, are the remains of plants and animals that lived thousands or millions of years ago.** (The two dependent clauses are underlined.)

Each dependent clause starts with words such as *after, although, who, which, when, until, where, so that,* and *since*. These clauses can tell *where, when,* and *why* something happened or can give more information about the people and things involved.

A. Understanding Complex Sentences

In each complex sentence below, find and underline the independent clauses with these words.

Scientists believe
Fossils have been found
Fossils indicate

Then underline each dependent clause twice.

1. Fossils have been found wherever scientists have searched hard.
2. Scientists believe that most species of plants and animals died out without leaving any fossils.
3. Fossils indicate that deserts were once sea bottoms.
4. Fossils that closely resemble living animals indicate that successful animals do not change much over time.
5. Because new evidence links birds and dinosaurs, scientists believe that birds may be the descendents of dinosaurs.
6. Although their exact age cannot be determined, fossils have been found in different layers of rock, which indicate relative ages.
7. Because nests of baby dinosaurs have been found, scientists believe that these ancient creatures cared for their young for some time.
8. Even though we cannot guess at the colors of prehistoric flowers, fossils indicate that flowering plants date from about 138 million years ago.

B. Understanding Complex Sentences

In each of these complex sentences, underline only the independent clause.

1. Since Eldon hates airplanes, he'll probably take the train even though it is slow.
2. If you see Rita, please tell her to return my lunchbox that she borrowed last week.
3. Someone forgot to water the roses that grow in the side yard.
4. Wherever you go, you'll find interesting people whom you can write about.
5. Although the farmer is ready, the ground is still too wet to plow.

Name ______________________ Date ______

Lesson 3

Complex Sentences

More Practice

A. Understanding Complex Sentences

In each of these complex sentences, underline each independent clause once and each dependent clause twice.

1. Until you change those strings, your banjo won't sound very good.
2. Darryl looked after my dog while I was away.
3. Bring your backpack when you come to school today.
4. When my grandmother was young, she listened to Frank Sinatra records.
5. Unless I am wrong, peaches were first grown in China.
6. Linda will lend Wei the book when she has finished it.
7. The announcer whose voice is so pleasant has switched to the morning drive time.
8. Write about your experience while it is still fresh in your mind.
9. In this plan, you pay as you go.
10. None of the poems that I like best are in this anthology.

B. Identifying Kinds of Sentences

Identify each sentence below with **S** for simple, **CD** for compound, or **CX** for complex.

1. Scientists can determine the relative age of fossils from the layers of rock in which the fossils are found. ______
2. Fossils in lower layers are older; those in higher layers are younger. ______
3. The oldest fossils of any group of living things are simpler than the more recent fossils are. ______
4. To scientists, this is clear evidence that plants and animals change over time. ______
5. The oldest fossils are approximately 3.5 billion years old. ______
6. These ancient fossils are traces of bacteria, which are one-celled organisms. ______
7. Animals without backbones came into being about 700 million years ago, but animals with backbones did not appear until about 500 million years ago. ______
8. If you could travel in time, would you go to the time of the dinosaurs? ______
9. Even the air must have smelled different that long ago! ______

Name ________________________________ Date ______________

Lesson 3

Compl[…] Sentences

Application

A. Cre[…]ing Complex Sentences

Comb[…] each numbered sentence with the first sentence that follows to make a co[…]lex sentence. Add, drop, or change words as needed. Write the new […]entences below.

(1) Evidence from fossils shows something. The continents have changed shape and position. **(2)** Dinosaurs appeared about 240 million years ago. All the continents were connected. **(3)** Fossils of mammals are very different from continent to continent. Mammals appeared about 40 million years later. **(4)** The first mammals lived about 200 million years ago. The continents had begun to split apart by that time.

1. ____

____

2. ____

____

3. ____

____

4. ____

____

B. Revising Complex Sentences

Underline the independent clause in each of these complex sentences. Then rewrite the sentence, keeping the independent clause but supplying a new dependent clause.

1. We ate the fruit because we were hungry.

____

2. After the curtain accidentally fell during her speech, the actress forgot her lines.

____

____

3. A statue that was sculpted by Rodin is on display at the museum.

____

____

Name ______________________________ Date ____________

Lesson 4

Kinds of Dependent Clauses

Teaching

An **adjective clause** is a dependent clause that is used as an adjective. An adjective clause modifies a noun or pronoun. It tells *what kind, which one, how much,* or *how many.*

Rosa likes furniture that was made in colonial America. (*Which* furniture?)

Adjective clauses are usually joined to the main clause by **relative pronouns** such as *who, whom, whose, that,* and *which.* A clause beginning with *which* is set off by commas.

This antiques dealer, who has similar pieces, has reasonable prices. (describes *dealer)*
This chair, which Rosa bought recently, was made about 1720. (describes *chair)*

An **adverb clause** is a dependent clause that is used as an adverb. It modifies a verb, adjective, or adverb. Adverb clauses tell *where, when, how, why, under what conditions,* and *to what extent.*

Because such chairs are rare, they are valuable. (tells *why,* modifies verb)

Adverb clauses are usually joined to the main clause by **subordinating conjunctions** such as *if, because, although, as, when, where,* and *while.*

A **noun clause** is a dependent clause used as a noun. Noun clauses may be used anywhere in a sentence that nouns can be used.

Subject	Who made the furniture is not known.
Direct Object	Rosa buys whatever antiques she can afford.
Predicate Nominative	This table is what she found last year.

Usually, a noun clause is joined to the main clause by words such as *who, whom, whoever, whomever, that, which, what, when, how, where, why,* and *whether.*

Identifying Adjective, Adverb, and Noun Clauses

Write **ADJ** (adjective), **ADV** (adverb), or **N** (noun) to identify each boldfaced clause.

1. Duncan Phyfe was an American furniture designer **who lived from 1768 to 1854.** ______
2. Phyfe came to America from Scotland, **where he was born.** ______
3. **When Phyfe came to America,** he settled in New York City. ______
4. The style **that Phyfe made popular** is called the Federal style. ______
5. **What made Phyfe famous** was his chairs and seats. ______
6. His chairs have backs **that are shaped like scrolls.** ______
7. Phyfe took ideas from neoclassical style, **because that was popular in England.** ______
8. Americans still admired **whatever the English admired.** ______
9. The neoclassical style was introduced in England by Robert Adam, **who was also from Scotland.** ______
10. A furniture style that began in France was **what inspired Adam.** ______

Name ______________________ Date ______________

Lesson 4

Kinds of Dependent Clauses

More Practice

A. Identifying Adjective, Adverb, and Noun Clauses

In each sentence, underline the dependent clause. On the line, write **ADJ** (adjective), **ADV** (adverb), or **N** (noun) to identify the clause.

EXAMPLE I simply like furniture that is comfortable. *ADJ*

1. The art museum has an exhibit of furniture that came from ancient Egypt. ______
2. That throne, which belonged to King Tutankhamen, is one of the loveliest pieces. ______
3. What the average Egyptian of that time had in his or her home was only a simple stool or two. ______
4. Because the furniture is so old, the museum controls the humidity in the hall. ______
5. If you had lived in classical Greece, you probably would have slept on the floor. ______
6. Whoever was rich enough had an elegant bed. ______
7. Many Greek tables had three legs that ended in feet shaped like paws. ______
8. Romans borrowed Greek furniture styles, as they borrowed most Greek things. ______
9. Although the Romans began with the same styles, they adapted them. ______
10. Today we still use styles that were developed by the Romans. ______

B. Identifying Clauses and Their Roles

Underline once the dependent clause in each sentence. If that clause is an adjective or an adverb clause, write on the line the word it modifies. If the clause is a noun clause, write **S, O,** or **PN** to tell whether the clause is used as the subject of a verb, direct or indirect object of a verb or object of a preposition, or a predicate nominative.

1. That loud girl on the bus said whatever popped into her head. ______
2. As I walked past the phone booth on the corner, the phone was ringing. ______
3. Did the mail carrier bring the letter that you were waiting for? ______
4. Whoever needs a pencil may take one from the storage cabinet. ______
5. Close all of the programs before you shut down the computer. ______
6. The city is reclaiming land around the factory, which was contaminated by the waste products. ______
7. Until we hear from the contest judges, we will be holding our breath. ______

Name ______________________________ Date ______________

Kinds of Dependent Clauses

Application

A. Identifying Adjective, Adverb, and Noun Clauses

Each sentence has at least one dependent clause. Underline each dependent clause, and, next to the underlined words, write **ADJ** (adjective), **ADV** (adverb), or **N** (noun) to identify its type.

1. One of the characteristics that made classic Chinese furniture remarkable was how the craftspeople joined the parts without pegs, nails, or even glue.

2. Because Japan is subject to frequent earthquakes, Japanese furniture has consisted of small, lightweight pieces that can easily be moved to safety.

3. Although a stool is smaller than a throne, in Ghana and other parts of Africa, it had the same role, because the stool was reserved for whoever was chief.

4. *Cassones* are large chests that were made by craftspeople who worked in Italy in the period between 1300 and 1600, which is called the *Renaissance*.

B. Using Dependent Clauses

Rewrite each sentence with a clause that fits the description in parentheses.

1. (Noun clause, subject of the verb *sang*) He sang with the orchestra.

____

2. (Adjective clause, modifying *radio*) I turned off the radio.

____

3. (Adverb clause, modifying *strong*) The wind was strong.

____

4. (Noun clause, object of *about*) The club members talked about it.

____

5. (Adverb clause, telling *when*) Did you have a good time?

____

Name ______________________ Date ____________

Compound-Complex Sentences

Teaching

A **compound-complex sentence** has two or more independent clauses and one or more dependent clauses.

> The Great Barrier Reef that lies off the coast of Australia is the largest in the world; the reef off the coast of Belize is the largest in the Western Hemisphere.

A. Identifying Clauses

In each compound-complex sentence below, the dependent clause is underlined. Identify the sentence parts named in the parentheses. Write the sentence parts on the line.

1. Before the Spanish conquered Peru, the Incas had built a walled city called Machu Picchu; this tour visits the ruins of that city.

   (simple subject and verb of the first independent clause) ____________

   (simple subject and verb of the second independent clause) ____________

2. The Grand Canyon is a stunning sight, but Yosemite National Park also has many impressive features that you will never forget.

   (simple subject and verb of the first independent clause) ____________

   (simple subject and verb of the dependent clause) ____________

3. New Orleans is known for its lively French Quarter, and visitors who have an interest in history will enjoy a tour of the historic sites.

   (simple subject and verb of the dependent clause) ____________

   (simple subject and verb of the second independent clause) ____________

B. Identifying Kinds of Sentences

Identify each sentence below with **CD** for compound, **CX** for complex, or **CD-CX** for compound-complex.

1. Stay a little longer if you like. ______
2. Although my dog can play the piano, he does not do it well, and nobody asks him for encores. ______
3. After the last song, the musicians packed up their instruments and got on the bus. ______
4. No one should ride on a motorcycle unless he or she wears a helmet. ______
5. I'll go if I can, but several events are scheduled for that day. ______
6. Spring came and went quickly, but I was ready for summer. ______
7. When you called, I was reading a book; now I can't find my place. ______

Name ______________________________ Date ______________

Lesson 5

Compound-Complex Sentences

More Practice

A. Identifying Clauses

In each compound-complex sentence below, draw parentheses around each independent clause and underline each dependent clause.

1. A tourist attraction that also has practical importance is the Panama Canal; both cruise ships and freighters pass through it daily.
2. Is the Sears Tower in Chicago still the tallest building in the world, or have any buildings that have gone up recently taken that honor?
3. When the last tsar of Russia was arrested by revolutionaries, he and his family were hiding at a palace near St. Petersburg; now that palace is open to tourists.
4. Mount Fuji in Japan has become so popular with tourists that crowding has become a real problem, but I would still like to travel there.
5. You can take a large cruise ship to see the glaciers of Alaska, or you can ride a smaller boat that can go closer to the coast and its icy covering.
6. I'd like to see the North Pole, but I will never go where it is that cold!

B. Identifying Kinds of Sentences

Identify each sentence below with **S** for simple, **CD** for compound, **CX** for complex, or **CD-CX** for compound-complex.

1. My aunt has joined an investment club that investigates and buys stocks, and she has made a little profit already. ______
2. The Great Barrier Reef forms a natural breakwater for the coast of northeast Australia and attracts tourists from all over the world. ______
3. Just thinking is not enough; you must think of something. ______
4. We had gone only a little way into the cave before our flashlight went out. ______
5. Although snow was predicted, the temperature has stayed above freezing, so rain is falling instead. ______
6. Is the universe expanding, or is it contracting? ______
7. After the holiday dinner is over, my brother washes dishes and I dry them. ______
8. The last car of the poky old freight train is just now coming into view. ______
9. Everyone who saw the movie has liked it, so I'm going tonight. ______
10. We tried hard, but the job was harder than we expected. ______

Name ______________________________ Date ______________

Lesson 5

Compound-Complex Sentences

Application

A. Identifying Kinds of Sentences

Identify each sentence below with **S** for simple, **CD** for compound, **CX** for complex, or **CD-CX** for compound-complex.

1. San Francisco is built on hills, and some of the streets are quite steep. ______
2. Because almost all parts of Hawaii are almost always cooled by winds, visitors rarely complain about the heat. ______
3. In Florida, if you aren't a fan of amusement parks, you can explore the Everglades, or you can go to the beaches, which are a fine place to relax. ______
4. Visitors to Pennsylvania can explore historic sites of the Revolutionary War at Valley Forge or of the Civil War at Gettysburg. ______

B. Writing Different Kinds of Sentences

Write compound-complex sentences by adding to the sentences in Exercise A according to the directions in parentheses.

1. (Locate the compound-complex sentence in Exercise A. Replace either independent clause.)

____

____

____

2. (Locate the compound sentence in Exercise A. Add an adjective clause.)

____

____

____

3. (Locate the complex sentence in Exercise A. Add another independent clause that tells another effect of the dependent clause.)

____

____

____

4. (Locate the simple sentence in Exercise A. Add an adverb clause that tells when, and another independent clause that tells about another state. Use a semicolon to join the second independent clause to the sentence.)

____

____

____

Name ______________________________ Date ______________

Agreement in Number

Teaching

CHAPTER 9

A verb must agree with its subject in number. **Number** refers to whether a word is singular—naming one—or plural—naming more than one.

A singular subject takes a singular verb.

That **boy** **follows** a trail. (singular subject, singular verb)

A plural subject takes a plural verb.

Those **boys** **follow** a trail. (plural subject, plural verb)

In a sentence with a verb phrase, the first helping verb must agree with the subject.

For the past hour the **boys** **have been following** the trail.

The **contractions** *doesn't* and *don't* are short forms of *does not* and *do not.* Use *doesn't* with all singular subjects except *I* and *you.* Use *don't* with all plural subjects, *I,* and *you.*

Doesn't this **tree** look old? **Don't** those **trees** look tall?

A. Making Subjects and Verbs Agree in Number

In each sentence, underline the subject. Then underline the verb in parentheses that agrees with the subject.

1. The turtles (was, were) sunning themselves on a log.
2. Marie (was, were) looking for dragonflies.
3. Her teacher (want, wants) her to write a paper on them.
4. Arthur (sketches, sketch) in his notebook.
5. Anna and Marie (has, have) never seen cattails before.
6. The teacher (says, say) cattails are edible.
7. They (was, were) disappointed when they tried eating one.
8. Jim (has, have) captured a garter snake.
9. He (assures, assure) everyone that it is not poisonous.
10. Fred (is, are) calling it a "garden snake."

B. Identifying Subjects and Verbs That Agree in Number

In each sentence, underline the subject and circle the verb. On the line following the sentence, write whether the two parts of the sentence **Agree** or **Disagree** in number.

1. Fred and John wants adventure on this hike. ______________
2. They is grabbing at a turtle. ______________
3. Their teacher reminds them of their promise not to remove any plants or animals. ______________
4. The students has agreed to that rule. ______________
5. The turtles have disappeared under the water. ______________

Name ________________________ Date ____________

Lesson 1

Agreement in Number

More Practice

CHAPTER 9

A. Making Subjects and Verbs Agree in Number

On the line following each sentence, write the present tense form of the verb that agrees with the subject.

1. The captain (board) the ship early this evening. ____________

2. The musicians (practice) diligently. ____________

3. Usually, the plumber (arrive) on the work site before the carpenter. ____________

4. The French teacher (like) browsing through bookstores. ____________

5. Tom (be) searching for a quote from Shakespeare. ____________

6. Fritz (think) the pasta dish is delicious. ____________

7. The team members (go) to the library together. ____________

8. Thomas (have) been working on that problem for a half hour. ____________

9. I (be) the one who spoke up when nobody else would. ____________

10. Marty (feel) she knows the piece well enough now. ____________

B. Correcting Agreement Errors

In each sentence, underline the subject and circle the verb. If the verb agrees with the subject, write **Correct** on the line to the right. If it does not agree, write the correct verb.

1. Jose are searching for leopard frogs. ____________

2. Mary were looking among the bushes. ____________

3. I were observing the water striders. ____________

4. They actually stand on the water surface. ____________

5. Their feet makes little indentations on the surface. ____________

6. How many students is on that bus? ____________

7. They were told to bring their lunches. ____________

8. One student have brought a net. ____________

9. How many sets of wings do dragonflies have? ____________

10. How do dragonflies and damselflies differ? ____________

Name ______________________________ Date ______________

Agreement in Number

Application

A. Proofreading for Errors in Agreement

Underline the five verbs in this paragraph that do not agree with their subjects. On the lines below, write the numbers of the sentences in which you find agreement errors. After each sentence number, write the subject and the verb form that agrees with it.

(1) Mr. Johnson love swamps. **(2)** Therefore, on our field trip we went to Green Swamp. **(3)** Most of us would have chosen a day at the beach. **(4)** According to Mr. Johnson, the neatest things happens in swamps. **(5)** He have lectured more than once on the topic of metamorphosis. **(6)** His examples has been caterpillars turning into butterflies and tadpoles turning into frogs. **(7)** He gets pretty excited about tadpoles. **(8)** Actually, the metamorphosis is amazing. **(9)** One week the animals are breathing with gills, like fish; and the next week they have lungs, like us. **(10)** Even the dedicated beach goers wants another visit to the swamp this fall.

____

____

____

____

____

B. Making Subjects and Verbs Agree in Writing

Choose one of the topics below and write a paragraph of at least four sentences about it. Use the present tense throughout. Make sure the subjects and verbs of all the sentences agree.

Exploring a swamp
A memorable field trip
Animals and plants in a swamp
Useful insects
Exploring a forest
Science class
Respect for nature
Tadpoles and frogs

____

____

____

____

____

____

____

Name ________________________________ Date ______________

Lesson 2

Compound Subjects

Teaching

A **compound subject** is made up of two or more simple subjects joined by a conjunction such as *and, or,* or *nor.*

And A compound subject whose subjects are joined by *and* usually takes a plural verb.

Monet and Manet **were** both great painters.

Sometimes a compound subject joined by *and* is used as a single unit and takes a singular verb.

The horse and buggy **is** an outmoded form of travel.

Or* or *Nor When the parts of a compound subject are joined by *or* or *nor,* the verb should agree with the part closest to it.

Neither the Impressionists nor Picasso **was** represented in that gallery.
Either Picasso or the Impressionists **are** good subjects for a term paper.

Making Verbs Agree with Compound Subjects

In each sentence, underline each part of the compound subject. Underline twice the word joining the parts. Then underline the verb in parentheses that agrees with the subject.

1. Both Vincent Van Gogh and Pablo Picasso (was, were) great artists.
2. Picasso and Diego Velázquez (was, were) Spanish.
3. Neither the sketches nor the painting (captures, capture) the subject completely.
4. Either the artist or the patron (is, are) going to be present.
5. The painters and sculptors (were, was) in agreement.
6. The patrons and the artist (has, have) been conferring on the project.
7. Neither the patrons nor the artist (has, have) been entirely happy.
8. Both Paul Cézanne and Picasso (are, is) major figures.
9. Paintings and music (works, work) well together.
10. Neither fine paintings nor memorable music (is, are) created easily.
11. Either Impressionist music or paintings (is, are) to be discussed in today's lecture.
12. The musicians and the artists (is, are) invited to the reception.
13. Neither the artists nor the director (is, are) responsible for the hors d'oeuvres.
14. Both the musicians and the artist (deserve, deserves) our thanks.
15. Either the gallery director or the artists (is, are) at the center of that crowd.
16. The patrons and guests (is, are) already anticipating next year's event.

Name ______________________ Date ______________

Compound Subjects

More Practice

A. Making Verbs Agree with Compound Subjects

In each sentence, underline each part of the compound subject. Underline twice the word joining the parts. Then underline the verb in parentheses that agrees with the subject.

1. The Wongs and the Sterlings (is, are) friends.
2. Neither the players nor the coach (feels, feel) ready for this game.
3. My mother and my father (agrees, agree) on the things that matter.
4. Either two socks or one shirt (fits, fit) in the pocket of the overnight bag.
5. Several students and the teacher (has, have) asked for new lights.
6. Either the students or the teacher (is, are) expected to be at the meeting.
7. Neither Teresa nor her brothers (talks, talk) very much.
8. Both the bikes and the moped (needs, need) new parts.
9. Either canned goods or money (is, are) an acceptable donation.
10. Dave's pet squirrel or the birds (taps, tap) at the window almost every hour.

B. Using the Correct Verb with a Compound Subject

Write the correct form of the given verb. Make it agree with the compound subject.

1. Neither the council members nor the mayor (be) present. ______________
2. Books and videotapes (be) available from the library. ______________
3. Both the council members and the mayor (have) spoken out on that matter. ______________
4. Neither the council members nor the mayor (object) to the proposal. ______________
5. Either the French horn or the trumpets (play) the next passage. ______________
6. The exercise book and tapes (come) from the library. ______________
7. Neither the glasses nor the bottle (be) full. ______________
8. The librarian or our history teachers (help) us find materials. ______________
9. Either the teachers or the librarian (be) helping Jack right now. ______________
10. Neither the reporters nor the photographer (come) to these meetings. ______________

CHAPTER 9

Name ______________________ Date ________

Lesson 2

Compound Subjects

Application

A. Correcting Errors in Agreement

Find the mistakes in the paragraph. For each sentence, write the correct present tense verb to agree with the subject. If the verb does agree, write **Correct.**

(1) The Impressionists and Post-Impressionists is the most important artists represented in our gallery. **(2)** Other galleries have bigger collections, but we have exceptional works in these two areas. **(3)** Neither the cubists nor Matisse are represented. **(4)** But either our Monet landscapes or our Degas self-portrait make us a center of modern art. **(5)** Both the landscape and the self-portrait is great.

1. ______________________

2. ______________________

3. ______________________

4. ______________________

5. ______________________

B. Using the Correct Verb with Compound Subjects

Write a sentence using each compound subject given in parentheses and a verb in the present tense. Add words to the given subject as needed for the sense of the sentence.

1. (a mother and her baby) ______________________

____

2. (several houses or a mall) ______________________

____

3. (Either art or music) ______________________

____

4. (several paintings or a sculpture) ______________________

____

5. (both the students and the teacher) ______________________

____

6. (a painting or two sketches) ______________________

____

Name ______________________________ Date ______________

Agreement Problems in Sentences *Teaching*

Subjects in Unusual Positions In questions, sentences beginning with *here* or *there,* or sentences in which an adjective, an adverb, or a phrase is placed first, the subject can be hard to find. Reorder the words in standard order to determine whether the verb should be singular or plural.

Question	**Does** your **house** have a big yard? Your **house does have** a big yard.
Here **and** ***There***	Here **are** the new **bushes.** The new **bushes are** here.
Beginning Phrase	Beyond the hedge **lies** a **fishpond.** A **fishpond lies** beyond the hedge.

Predicate Nouns A **predicate noun** follows a linking verb and describes the subject. The verb must agree with the subject, not the predicate noun.

The **delight** of the gardener **is** the old rosebushes.
The old **rosebushes are** the gardener's delight.

Prepositional Phrases The subject of a verb is never part of a prepositional phrase. Mentally block out any words between the subject and verb. Make the verb agree with the subject.

This **pot** ~~of flowers~~ **blooms** in spring. (singular subject and verb)
The **flowers** ~~in this pot~~ **bloom** in spring. (plural subject and verb)

Making Subjects and Verbs Agree

Underline the subject of each sentence. Draw a line through any phrase that separates the subject from the verb. Finally, underline the verb that agrees with the subject.

1. Houses by Frank Lloyd Wright (is, are) usually on the National Register.
2. (Does, Do) the inexperienced actors in the play know their lines?
3. The students in the honors class (is, are) doing a new project.
4. Movies full of intrigue and adventure (appeals, appeal) to Henry.
5. Off through the woods (runs, run) Little Red Riding Hood.
6. Meals on the road (is, are) a problem.
7. (Does, Do) this restaurant's fish sandwiches taste fishy?
8. Only one can of chicken-with-rice soup (is, are) left on the shelf.
9. "Off with their heads," (shouts, shout) the mad queen.
10. There (is, are) ten eggs still in the refrigerator.
11. (Is, Are) the students' parents invited to the reception?
12. The list of names of donors (is, are) being read now.
13. Down the river (rushes, rush) the racing canoes.
14. (Has, Have) the famous architect visited her completed homes?

Name ______________________________ Date ______________

Lesson 3

Agreement Problems in Sentences

More Practice

CHAPTER 9

A. Making Subjects and Verbs Agree

Underline the subject. Then underline the verb that agrees with the subject.

1. (Is, Are) John and Marie going on the architectural tour?
2. Here (is, are) a building and a gardener's cottage by Frank Lloyd Wright.
3. Maintenance of these older buildings (is, are) difficult.
4. The number of buildings from the 1920s (falls, fall) yearly.
5. (Do, Does) Wright's office building still exist?
6. There (stands, stand) the Adler and Sullivan skyscraper.
7. (Was, Were) Wright working for Louis Sullivan at that time?
8. The list of remarkable structures (is, are) a long one.
9. Here (is, are) one of the first major buildings by Henry Hobson Richardson.
10. Where (was, were) Richardson living then?

B. Correcting Agreement in Number

In each of these sentences, decide whether the verb agrees with the subject. If it does, write **Correct** on the line. If it does not, write the correct form of the verb on the line.

1. Were the exchange student taking English as a second language? ______
2. There was seven ducks in the pond this afternoon. ______
3. Here are the list of books for my biology class. ______
4. Up into the clouds soar the skyscrapers. ______
5. Aren't Aunt Emily a music teacher? ______
6. Have you seen the newly opened apartment building? ______
7. Who construct such large buildings as this one? ______
8. Arsonists is the cause of this terrible fire. ______
9. From the ashes of the burned block rises a new neighborhood. ______
10. There is no Stanford White buildings here. ______
11. A problem for the plumbing and electrical departments are vandals. ______
12. Yes, vandals are always a problem. ______

Name ______________________________ Date ____________

Agreement Problems in Sentences

Application

A. Correcting Agreement in Number

Underline the subject and verb of each numbered sentence. If there is an agreement error, write the subject and the correct form of the verb on the lines below. If the subject and verb agree, write **Correct.**

(1) Louis Sullivan, along with his partner Dankmar Adler, are considered the inventor of the skyscraper. **(2)** The ability to use steel girders by the end of the 1800s were a factor in this development. **(3)** No longer were a massive stone understructure necessary under the upper levels of a building. **(4)** From then on, the walls of a building could be considered just a "skin" covering the steel girders. **(5)** The decoration of the "skins" of Louis Sullivan buildings are usually one of their more noteworthy aspects.

1. ______________________________

2. ______________________________

3. ______________________________

4. ______________________________

5. ______________________________

B. Making Subjects and Verbs Agree

In each sentence beginning below, underline the word that should be used as the simple subject in a sentence. Then supply a complete predicate, including a verb of your choice, to complete the sentence. Make sure your verb agrees with the underlined subject.

Example The children at the table *are writing their book reports.*

1. A box of pens

____

2. The principal of the high school

____

3. The house with the blue shutters

____

4. That firm of lawyers

____

5. The pieces of the puzzle

____

CHAPTER 9

Name ______________________________ Date ______________

Lesson 4

Indefinite Pronouns as Subjects *Teaching*

An **indefinite pronoun** does not refer to a specific, person, place, thing, or idea.

When used as subjects, some indefinite pronouns are always singular. Others are always plural. Others can be singular or plural depending on how they are used.

Indefinite Pronouns					
Always Singular	another anybody anyone anything	each either everybody everyone	everything neither nobody no one	nothing one somebody someone	something
Always Plural	both	few	many	several	
Singular or Plural	all	any	most	none	some

Singular indefinite pronouns take singular verbs.

Neither of the books I wanted **was** in the library.

Plural indefinite pronouns take plural verbs.

Many of the videotapes **are** new.

All, any, most, none, and *some* can be singular or plural. If the pronoun refers to a single person or thing, it takes a singular verb. If it refers to more than one person or thing, it takes a plural verb.

All of these books **were** approved. (The books are considered as individual items.)
All of the reading list **was** approved. (The list is considered as one quantity.)

Making Indefinite Pronouns and Verbs Agree

In each sentence, underline the indefinite pronoun used as subject. If the pronoun changes number according to the noun it refers to, underline that noun. Then find the verb. If the verb agrees with the subject, write **Correct.** If not, write the correct verb form.

EXAMPLE Some of the speakers was students. *were*

1. All of the materials in this section is nonfiction. ______
2. Both of the librarians are willing to help. ______
3. Each of the librarians has years of experience. ______
4. Some of the magazines were bound. ______
5. A few of the finalists has been chosen. ______
6. Nobody among the students is allowed to eat lunch in the library. ______
7. Several of the students has used the unabridged dictionary already. ______
8. Either of the girls were allowed in the storeroom. ______
9. Most of my friends are excited about the news. ______
10. Is any of those science fiction books by Isaac Asimov? ______

Name ______________________________ Date ____________

Indefinite Pronouns as Subjects

More Practice

CHAPTER 9

A. Making Verbs Agree with Indefinite Pronoun Subjects

In each sentence, underline the indefinite pronoun used as subject. If the pronoun changes number according to the noun it refers to, also underline that noun. Then find the verb. If the verb agrees with the subject, write **Correct.** If not, write the correct verb form.

1. Was any of the athletes in the speech competition? ____________

2. Most of the neighbors was out of town. ____________

3. Several of the students are named in the article. ____________

4. All of the customers was getting impatient. ____________

5. A few of the council members were unwilling to go on record. ____________

6. One of the quarterbacks have been out sick. ____________

7. Several of the authors has spoken to the group. ____________

8. Has any of my friends called? ____________

9. Both of the clerks were helping customers. ____________

10. None of the cookies is chocolate. ____________

B. Using Verbs with Indefinite Pronoun Subjects

On the lines, write the correct present tense form of the verb for each sentence.

(1) Some of my friends (help) in their neighborhood library. **(2)** If any of you readers (think) this is boring, you would be surprised. **(3)** One of my friends (know) plenty about computers. She helps patrons use the computerized card catalog and the computer programs. **(4)** Another of the volunteers (prefer) to help shelve books. **(5)** All of Rosina's time (be) spent putting books back on the shelves.

1. ______________________________

2. ______________________________

3. ______________________________

4. ______________________________

5. ______________________________

Name ________________________________ Date ______________

Lesson 4

Indefinite Pronouns as Subjects

Application

CHAPTER 9

A. Checking Agreement of Verbs with Indefinite Pronoun Subjects

Proofread this paragraph for errors in subject-verb agreement. Underline any verb that does not agree with the indefinite pronoun used as its subject. On the lines below, write the number of each sentence with an error and rewrite the sentence correctly.

(1) One of my favorite pastimes are going to the library. **(2)** All of the books, magazines, and CDs I can't afford is there to borrow and use. **(3)** Some of the library materials is outside my areas of interest or understanding. **(4)** But many of the library's holdings refer to areas I know or would like to learn something about. **(5)** Everything are there. **(6)** And everybody with a library card are welcome to use it.

____

____

____

____

____

____

B. Using Verbs Correctly with Indefinite Pronouns as Subjects

In each sentence beginning below, underline the word that should be used as the simple subject in a sentence. Then supply a complete predicate, including a verb of your choice, to complete the sentence. Make sure your verb agrees with the underlined subject.

Example Some of the books *have been checked out.*

1. Most of the cars

2. All of the tables

3. None of the coffee

4. Both of the visitors

5. Either of the drivers

6. All of the snow

7. Some of the scientists

8. Most of the pool

Name ______________________ Date __________

Problem Subjects

Teaching

It may be difficult to tell whether the subjects in the following cases are singular or plural.

Collective Nouns A **collective noun** names a group of people or things. Examples include *group, team, family, class,* and *majority.* When the members act together, the collective noun takes a singular verb. When they act as individuals, it takes a plural verb.

Usually, the majority **is** satisfied with election results. (acting together)
The majority of the voters **are** young people. (acting as individuals)

Singular Nouns Ending in *S* Some nouns ending in *-s* or *-ics* appear to be plural but are considered singular. As subjects, these nouns take singular verbs. Examples include *news, measles, mumps, civics, mathematics, acoustics, physics,* and *molasses.*

For me, physics **is** difficult.

Titles Titles of works of art, literature, or music are singular.

The Thousand and One Nights **is** a collection of stories.

Time and Amounts Words and phrases that identify weights, measures, numbers, and time are usually considered singular. Fractions are considered singular or plural, depending on whether the subject is thought of as a whole or as separate objects.

Ten dollars **is** the usual ticket price. (singular)
Two days **is** the minimum time needed for delivering a letter. (singular)
Only three-fourths of the students **are** healthy. (plural)

CHAPTER 9

Using Verbs That Agree with Problem Subjects

In each sentence, underline the subject and the form of the verb that agrees with it.

1. Four tablespoons of butter (is, are) what the recipe calls for.
2. The soccer team (has, have) won the championship.
3. The soccer team (is, are) putting on their cleats.
4. Sixty cents (is, are) the price of a program
5. Only half of the club members (is, are) present.
6. According to an old saying, half of a loaf (is, are) better than none.
7. Measles (is, are) a painful illness.
8. Twelve dollars (is, are) enough for two dinners.
9. *The Gleaners* (is, are) a peaceful painting by Jean-Françoise Millet.
10. The family (is, are) having a reunion this summer.
11. The family (is, are) coming in from all points of the compass.
12. Two tons (equals, equal) four thousand pounds.
13. Mathematics (is, are) my favorite subject.
14. *Twice-Told Tales* (was, were) written by Hawthorne.
15. Molasses (is, are) an ingredient in baked beans.

Name ______________________________ Date __________

Lesson 5

Problem Subjects

More Practice

A. Using Verbs That Agree with Problem Subjects

In each sentence, underline the verb that agrees in number with the subject.

1. *Twenty Thousand Leagues Under the Sea* (is, are) a novel by Jules Verne.
2. For my brother, physics (has, have) been more interesting than chemistry.
3. Two dollars (has, have) always been the maximum fine for children's books.
4. Three-eighths of the students (is, are) boys.
5. Sixteen (was, were) his lucky number.
6. Three-eighths of the cup (is, are) filled.
7. For me, mathematics (is, are) a required course next year.
8. (Is, Are) three-eighths more than one-half?
9. Paul Gauguin's *Breton Girls by the Sea* (shows, show) two barefoot girls.
10. Pediatrics (is, are) the specialty of doctors who treat children.

B. Correcting Subject-Verb Agreement

If the verb agrees with its subject, write **Correct** on the line. If it disagrees, write the correct form of the verb.

1. The class have decided where to go for its field trip. __________
2. *Innocents Abroad* were written by Mark Twain. __________
3. After her family's reunion in Ireland, Siobhan's family news has been international in character. __________
4. Four thousand dollars are a high price for a car in that condition. __________
5. The graduating class has received their caps and gowns. __________
6. One hundred sixty is divisible by four. __________
7. Two-thirds of the violinists is sick with the flu. __________
8. One-fifth of the graduating seniors have won scholarships. __________
9. Measles are a common childhood disease. __________
10. "The Three Little Pigs" are a classic children's tale. __________

Name ______________________ Date ____________

Problem Subjects

Application

A. Proofreading for Subject-Verb Agreement

Proofread this paragraph for errors in subject-verb agreement. Draw a line through each incorrect verb. Then draw this proofreading symbol ^ next to the word and write the correction above the error.

Our class have been reading some books that are a kind of early science fiction. Mark Twain's *The Prince and the Pauper* were really science fiction, based on the notion of time travel. Jules Verne's *Twenty Thousand Leagues Under the Sea* were written about the same time as Twain's work. Physics, at least with respect to underwater pressures and forces, are essential to the Verne work. Mathematics are important too. The crew of the *Nautilus* need to calculate underwater locations as well as water pressures.

B. Writing Sentences

Complete each of these sentences by adding a present-tense verb as described in the parentheses. Add any other needed words.

EXAMPLE Ninety cents *is enough for a cup of coffee.*

1. My mother's bridge club ______________________
2. "The Three Billy Goats Gruff" ______________________
3. Social studies ______________________
4. The football team ______________________
5. Six dollars and fifty cents ______________________
6. *Romeo and Juliet* ______________________

CHAPTER 9

Name ______________________________ Date ____________

People and Cultures

Teaching

CHAPTER 10

Follow these rules of capitalization:

- Capitalize people's names and initials.

  William C. Bryant **W. C. Handy**

- Capitalize titles and the abbreviations of titles used before personal names or in direct address. Capitalize the abbreviations of some titles when they follow a name.

  Professor Lee **Dr. Darren Ames** **Hello, Senator.** **Julia Bishop, M.D.**

- Capitalize titles of heads of state, royalty, or nobility only when they are used before a person's name or in place of a person's name. Do not capitalize titles when they are used without a proper name.

  Sir Winston Churchill
  The Prince of Monaco attended the dinner last night.
  The prince waved to the crowd.

- Capitalize the titles indicating family relationships only when the titles are used as names or parts of names. Do not capitalize a family name when it follows the person's name or is used without a proper name.

  Uncle Bill **Grandpa Joe** **Jerome, my cousin, is starting college.**

- Always capitalize the pronoun *I*.
- Capitalize the names of religions, sacred days, sacred writings, and deities. Do not capitalize the words *god* or *goddess* when they refer to a group of gods, as in ancient mythology.

  Islam **Easter** **Torah** **Isis**

- Capitalize the names of nationalities, languages, races, and some ethnic groups, and the adjectives formed from these names.

  Brazilian **Irish American** **Caucasian**

Capitalizing Names of People and Cultures

Underline the words that should be capitalized in each of the following sentences.

1. Susan, my cousin, knows all the words to the french national anthem.
2. After doctor brown checks your teeth, you can leave.
3. When I earn my doctorate, i will be called Mira glazer, ph.d.
4. What is the british spelling of the word *color?*
5. We found a tattered bible that used to belong to grandma margaret.
6. It seems that general george washington was a popular overnight guest.
7. Poet robert frost spoke at the inauguration of president john f. kennedy.
8. According to greek mythology, the goddess hera was the wife of the god zeus.
9. Our guide, mr. carlos j. lopez, jr., showed us around the mexican ruins.
10. Of all my uncles, uncle Wiley is the tallest.

Name ________________________________ Date ______________

Lesson 1

People and Cultures

More Practice

A. Capitalizing Names

Underline the letters that should be capitals in each of the following sentences. If the sentence is already correct, write **Correct.**

1. My friend marie plays the french horn in our local orchestra. __________

2. When aunt irene visited, we went with her to st. cyril byzantine Church. __________

3. How would you rate the bill's chance of passing, senator? __________

4. Where did eve learn to speak portuguese so fluently? __________

5. Did you see queen marie antoinette's dress in that drawing? __________

6. My dad and i have appointments with our dentist, edward klein, d.d.s. __________

7. We were in a restaurant with the governor when we visited the state capital. __________

8. The russian language is quite difficult to learn, or so i've been told. __________

9. When ms. heller and ms. jeffries get together, they have a great time. __________

10. One of my favorite greek myths is the creation story about the gods who were called the titans. __________

B. Capitalizing Correctly

Draw three lines under each lowercase letter that should be capitalized in the following paragraph.

(1) Harriet beecher stowe wrote a book that helped to change american history. **(2)** Her father, lyman beecher, was a presbyterian minister. **(3)** When reverend beecher moved to Cincinnati, Ohio, to serve as president of a seminary, harriet went along. **(4)** There she saw firsthand the problems of african slaves trying to escape to freedom. **(5)** After harriet married calvin stowe, she moved to Maine and began to write about her strong feelings against slavery. **(6)** The novel she wrote, *Uncle Tom's Cabin,* created strong emotions regarding the slavery issue. **(7)** Some people say that stowe's words were part of the reason the Civil War was fought. **(8)** In fact, when president abraham lincoln met her, he said, "So you're the little woman who wrote the book that made this great war!"

CHAPTER 10

Name ______________________________ Date ____________

Lesson 1

People and Cultures

Application

A. Proofreading

Proofread the following first draft of a report. Look especially for errors in capitalization. Draw three lines under each letter that should be capitalized.

Example Oliver wendell holmes was an american writer.

Oliver wendell holmes was a man of many talents and interests. He was a doctor, a writer, and a popular public speaker. Holmes was born in 1809 in Cambridge, Massachusetts. Oliver's father was a congregationalist minister. While reverend holmes was quite strict, oliver was more freethinking. Though oliver started law school, he quickly got bored. Instead, he went to Harvard Medical School. During his time at Harvard, he wrote poetry. Oliver's father, i am sure, was quite proud of his son. When oliver wendell holmes, m.d., graduated, he became an excellent doctor and the author of many articles about medical problems. One of his sons, oliver wendell holmes, jr., became a chief justice of the United States Supreme Court.

B. Writing with Capital Letters

The people of some islands in the Pacific Ocean used to have an interesting custom. When people met, they would introduce themselves by telling their own names and the names of their parents, grandparents, and other relatives. Write a conversation that two people might have when they meet on such an island. Include at least five complete names capitalized correctly.

CHAPTER 10

Name ____________________ Date ____________

First Words and Titles

Teaching

Capitalize these words:

- the first word of every sentence
- the first word of every line of traditional poetry
- the first word of a direct quotation if it is a complete sentence (Do not capitalize a direct quotation if it is a sentence fragment.) *Example:* "What is your favorite book of all time?" asked Ms. Barton.

  Do not capitalize the first word of the second part of a divided quotations unless it starts a new sentence. *Example:* "Let's think of the books," she said, "that we would recommend to others."
- the first word of each item in an outline and the letters that introduce major subsections
- the first word in the greeting of a letter and the first word in the closing
- the first word, the last word, and all other important words in titles (Don't capitalize articles, conjunctions, or prepositions of fewer than five letters.)

CHAPTER 10

Capitalizing First Words and Titles

Underline the words that should be capitalized in each of the following items.

1. "when you say book do you mean only novels?" asked Julie.
2. "Why?" asked her teacher. "what kind of writing would you include in addition to novels?"
3. Julie replied, "there are books filled with poems, essays, and short stories, too."
4. "for example," said Julie, "think about a book of Thomas Paine's essays."
5. one of his essays called *the american crisis* includes these stirring words: "these are the times that try men's souls."
6. "my favorite book," said Henry, "might be *a tale of two cities* by Charles Dickens."
7. "it begins this way: 'it was the best of times. it was the worst of times,'" Henry said.
8. here is the beginning of an outline of the books I would choose:

   I. nineteenth-century authors

      a. british authors

         1. works of Robert Louis Stevenson

         2. works of Charles Dickens
9. dear Ms. Barton,

   after I thought about it for a while, I decided that my favorite book is one that I read when I was little, *the lion, the witch, and the wardrobe.*

   your student,

   bill

Name ______________________________ Date ______________

First Words and Titles

More Practice

A. Capitalizing First Words and Titles

In the following sentences, underline the words that should be capitalized but are not. If the sentence contains no capitalization errors, write **Correct** on the line.

1. "after lunch," said Sasha, "let's walk uptown."

2. I have just finished reading *life on the mississippi*.

3. be sure to read my article "the mayoral election" in today's newspaper.

4. here he lies where he longed to be;
home is the sailor, home from the sea,
and the hunter, home from the hill.

—Robert Louis Stevenson, "Requiem"

5. "three may keep a secret," said Benjamin Franklin, "if two of them are dead."

6. our class will see a production of the play *romeo and juliet* at the playhouse.

7. what do you think of the saying that children should be "seen but not heard"?

8. "The egg of today," says a proverb, "is better than a hen of tomorrow."

9. have you ever heard the song "this land is your land"?

10. one of my favorite short stories is "the fall of the house of usher."

B. Capitalizing First Words in Outlines

Underline each letter that should be capitalized in the following outline.

Brazil

I. location

II. climate facts

a. average temperature in summer

b. average temperature in winter

c. average annual precipitation

III. the people

a. languages

b. religions

c. major cities

CHAPTER 10

Name ______________________ Date __________

First Words and Titles

Application

A. Writing a Conversation

Continue this conversation two people had after reading a good book. Have the two speakers compare this book (you can decide which book they both read) with other books they have read. Include at least two other book titles. Be sure to capitalize the quotations and titles correctly.

"How did you like the book we just finished?" asked Rita. "I thought it was great."

"I liked it, too. It reminded me of other books I have read," replied Brad.

____

____

____

____

____

____

B. Writing an Outline Using Capital Letters Correctly

Read the following brief report. Then write a short outline for it on the lines below. Be sure to capitalize correctly.

Robert Louis Stevenson was an author who lived an unusual life. As a child in Scotland, he was sickly. He had lung problems that kept him in bed quite a bit. When he was 17, he attended Edinburgh University and soon became a lawyer. But what he really loved to do was write.

Stevenson's health was poor throughout his life. In hopes of getting better, he moved from place to place. He especially loved the sea and spent years sailing his yacht around the South Seas. He got many of his ideas for his books such as *Treasure Island* and *Kidnapped* from his travels.

The Life of Robert Louis Stevenson

I. Early life

____

____

II. Later life

____

____

CHAPTER 10

Name ______________________ Date ____________

Lesson 3

Places and Transportation

Teaching

Follow these rules of capitalization:

- In geographical names, capitalize each word except articles and prepositions. Geographical names include the names of continents *(Asia)*, bodies of water *(Black Sea)*, islands *(Hawaiian Islands)*, mountains *(Rocky Mountains)*, other landforms *(Sahara Desert)*, world regions *(Midwest)*, nations *(Brazil)*, states *(Nebraska)*, cities *(Louisville)*, and streets *(Maple Street)*.
- Capitalize the names of planets and other specific objects in the universe.

  Jupiter **Andromeda Galaxy**

- Capitalize the words *north, south, east,* and *west* when they name particular regions of the country or world, or when they are parts of proper names. Do not capitalize words that indicate general directions or locations.

  South America **We drove south to New Orleans.**

- Capitalize the names of specific buildings, bridges, monuments, and other landmarks.

  Mount Rushmore **Brooklyn Bridge**

- Capitalize the names of specific airplanes, trains, ships, cars, and spacecraft.

  Mayflower ***Sputnik***

CHAPTER 10

Capitalizing Names and Places

Underline the words that should be capitalized in each of the following sentences. If the item is capitalized correctly, write **Correct** on the line.

1. Maybe someday I will visit england, france, and other countries of europe. ____________

2. In the past, people took ships like the *queen mary* to europe. ____________

3. That kind of travel is nice, but I would rather take a fast jet like the *concorde.* ____________

4. When I get to london, I want to visit the tower of london and buckingham palace. ____________

5. Maybe I'll pass by the official home of the prime ministers at 10 Downing Street. ____________

6. Is that address in the east, west, north, or south part of London? ____________

7. In France, I would go to the louvre museum. ____________

8. Did you ever hear how excited the people of paris were when Charles Lindbergh landed his plane, *spirit of st. louis,* near the city in 1927? ____________

9. I would like to see a sight like the planet venus over the famous eiffel tower in paris, too. ____________

Name ______________________ Date ____________

Places and Transportation *More Practice*

Lesson 3

A. Capitalizing Names and Places

Underline the words that should be capitalized in each of the following sentences. If the item is capitalized correctly, write **Correct** on the line.

1. On our trip to the west, we saw the geyser they call old faithful. ________
2. Early in June we plan to climb castle peak in colorado. ________
3. First we'll hike up from ashcroft and ski in montezuma basin. ________
4. Violent typhoons occur in the south china sea, which is really the western part of the pacific ocean. ________
5. The blue ridge parkway leads to great smoky mountains national park. ________
6. Was it *apollo 11* that blasted into outer space in 1969? ________
7. Did you know that the george washington bridge connects fort lee, new jersey, with new york city? ________
8. In 1934, the burlington *zephyr,* the first passenger train powered by a diesel-electric locomotive, began service. ________
9. Which planet has rings, saturn or jupiter? ________
10. In 1492, the *santa maria* arrived in the bahamas. ________
11. I wonder if I'll still be around the next time Halley's Comet is visible from Earth. ________
12. On a visit to the middle east, you can see the ancient city of jerusalem. ________

B. Capitalizing Names of Places in a Paragraph

Underline the words that should be capitalized in the following paragraph.

london, england, is one of the oldest cities in the world. Long ago, the city which we now call london was really two cities—the City of london and the City of westminster. The City of london started out as an outpost of the roman empire around A.D. 43. The City of westminster was built around 1,000 years later. Now london is so big that it includes both of the ancient cities and much more. In this huge city, you can see sights such as the london bridge over the thames river. You can visit famous places such as trafalgar square and piccadilly circus, which is really not a circus. Instead, it is a big traffic circle. In fact, since the traffic is so heavy in london, it's best not to drive at all. Most visitors travel around the city on the subway called the london underground.

CHAPTER 10

Name ______________________ Date ____________

Lesson 3

Places and Transportation

Application

A. Capitalizing Names of Places

On the lines, write a list of five real or imaginary places you would like to visit in your life. Write as much of the address of the place as you know. For some, you may know the street address, the city, the state, the country, the continent, the hemisphere, the planet, and the galaxy. For others, you may know only part of that information.

B. Using Capital Letters in Writing

Write a description of your hometown for a travel brochure. Mention important landmarks, main streets, nearby cities or towns, mountains, lakes, rivers, or oceans. Tell readers what they are likely to see, hear, or experience at some of those places. Try to make your city attractive to people who like to travel.

Name ______________________________ Date ______________

Organizations and Other Subjects *Teaching*

Use capital letters for the following:

- all of the important words in names of organizations, institutions, stores, and companies.

  Jackson Garden Club **Madison Middle School** **Village Market**

- names of historical events, periods, and documents

  War of the Roses **Mesozoic Era** **Treaty of Ghent**

- abbreviations B.C., A.D., A.M., and P.M.

  6:20 A.M. **130 B.C.**

- names of months, days, and holidays but not the names of seasons except when used as part of a festival or celebration

  Sunday, March 4 **Thanksgiving Day** **Annual Spring Concert**

- names of special events and awards

  Newbery Medal **Millersburg Festival**

- brand names of products but not a common noun that follows a brand name

  Cold Comfort ice-cream sandwich

Identifying Correct Capitalization

Underline the words or letters that should be capitals in each of the following sentences.

1. Students from mitchell middle school are studying the 19th century in their American history class.
2. They recently learned about a time known as the era of good feeling, when James Monroe was president.
3. President Monroe is also known for the monroe doctrine, a document that told the powers of Europe to keep their hands off the Western Hemisphere.
4. However, probably the most important event during the 19th century in the United States was the civil war.
5. The students read the famous gettysburg address, given by Abraham Lincoln at the gettysburg national cemetery.
6. On may 23, the school will have its american history celebration.
7. The winner will receive the mitchell history prize.
8. Entries such as videos, plays, and posters will be accepted until tuesday, may 22.
9. Judges from mitchell public library and mitchell city hall will judge the entries.
10. The prizes will be awarded at 8:00 p.m.; the winner will also get coupons for findaway maps from the local map store.

CHAPTER 10

Name ______________________ Date __________

Lesson 4

Organizations and Other Subjects *More Practice*

A. Capitalizing Names of Organizations and Other Subjects

Underline each letter that should be capitalized in the following sentences.

1. My sister is looking forward to valentine's day on february 14.
2. Some of us visited the museum of technology and industry on friday.
3. The holy roman empire was much weaker after the thirty years' war.
4. The university of danvers in Texas has a good law school.
5. How will the sanderson environmental club observe earth day?
6. In 1919 the treaty of versailles helped to end world war I.
7. Don't forget to buy me a wonder marker to use for my poster display.
8. In New Orleans people celebrate mardi gras with parades.
9. Last friday, Ms. Cummings started working for comfort shoes, inc.
10. This summer Carla joined the league of concerned voters.

B. Capitalizing Correctly

Rewrite every sentence that contains a capitalization error. If a sentence is capitalized correctly, write **Correct** on the line.

1. Is northern middle school near kennedy hospital?

____

2. The stephens planetarium will change its program in january.

____

3. I packed two pairs of Fitrite socks for the hiking trip this fall.

____

4. The spring prom begins on april 30 at 8:30 p.m. in the striker auditorium.

____

5. Will cleo press publish Joe's book about the great depression?

____

6. The fourth of july picnic is always fun.

____

7. Back in the middle ages, King John of England signed the magna carta.

____

CHAPTER 10

Name ______________________________ Date ____________

Lesson 4

Organizations and Other Subjects

Application

A. Proofreading for Capitalization Errors

Read the following speech given at a school awards ceremony. Draw three lines under any letters that should be capitalized but are not.

Example Welcome to our recognition day ceremony.

Revere middle school is proud to honor some of its students at this recognition day ceremony. The students we honor have helped their community in many ways—from serving turkey on thanksgiving day to reading to disabled veterans of the vietnam war. They have worked at the golden times nursing home and have given up their saturday mornings to tutor other students here at revere middle school. We are proud to award the revere community helpers award to these students. After the ceremony, please join us for punch and cookies in the cafeteria.

B. Using Capitalization in Writing

Write sentences that combine names from any two categories listed below. First tell the categories you have chosen. Then write your sentence.

organizations	institutions	stores	companies	historical events
historical periods	documents	days	months	holidays
	awards	brand names	time periods	
			abbreviations	

Example I am combining *brand names and time abbreviations.*
I wonder if people in 5000 B.C. would have liked Super shoes?

1. I am combining ____________ and ____________.

Sentence: ______________________________

2. I am combining ____________ and ____________.

Sentence: ______________________________

3. I am combining ____________ and ____________.

Sentence: ______________________________

4. I am combining ____________ and ____________.

Sentence: ______________________________

5. I am combining ____________ and ____________.

Sentence: ______________________________

CHAPTER 10

Name ______________________________ Date ______________

Lesson 1 Periods and Other End Marks *Teaching*

The three end marks are the **period, question mark,** and **exclamation point.**

Periods Use a period at the end of a **declarative sentence**—one that makes a statement.

The mayor is the top city official.

Use a period at the end of almost every **imperative sentence.** An imperative sentence gives a command. If a command is said with emotion, it ends in an exclamation point.

Please transfer me to the fire department!

Use a period at the end of an **indirect question.** An indirect question reports what a person asked without using the person's exact words.

I asked who has the job of dogcatcher.

Use a period after an **abbreviation** or an **initial,** as in this example: Mr. Nelson R. Diaz.

Use a period after each number and letter in an **outline** or **list.**

Question Marks Use a question mark to end an **interrogative sentence,** or question.

Who is the dogcatcher?

Exclamation Points Use an exclamation point to end an **exclamatory sentence,** a sentence that expresses strong feeling. Use an exclamation point after an **interjection** as well.

Wow! What an incredible victory that election gave us!

Using Periods and Other End Marks

Add punctuation as necessary in the following items.

1. The election is in six weeks
2. Mrs Joan T Reynolds is running against Mr Robert J Bachman, Jr
3. Imagine—we have two candidates with real credentials
4. Last time, neither candidate had experience
5. How difficult this choice will be
6. Polls open at 6 A M and close at 9 P M
7. The city will face several critical issues during the next four years
8. I Transportation
   A Rail traffic extensions
   B Bridge reconstructions
   II Delivery of services
   A Garbage and sanitation
   B Police and fire services

CHAPTER 11

Name ______________________________ Date ____________

Lesson 1

Periods and Other End Marks

More Practice

A. Using End Marks

Add punctuation marks where necessary in the following items.

1. A voter asked the candidates what their priorities and plans were
2. We won Hooray Happy days are here again
3. The issues are sewers, schools, and sprawl
4. Mr Thompson, the alderman, opposes any new taxes
5. The Town Board meets at 7:00 P M—sharp
6. Did you find out how the vote went
7. The "nay" votes will outnumber the "aye" votes
8. Do you plan to get up and talk
9. Tell me how you feel about the issues
10. Could you hear Alderman Morrissey's comment
11. I Issues facing the town in the next decade
    A Sewer extensions
    B School budget
    C Suburban sprawl
    D Taxes
    II Leaders
12. Hey I still have the floor

B. Using End Marks in Writing

Add the correct end mark at the end of each sentence in the following paragraph.

Americans are becoming more and more suspicious of public officials__ First-time candidates brag about never having held office__ Turn out the rascals__ Get rid of the scoundrels__ Those are the slogans of many campaigns__ But does this attitude make sense__ We should never assume that officeholders are incompetent __ Instead, we must insist on honest work__

CHAPTER 11

Name ______________________ Date ____________

Lesson 1

Periods and Other End Marks

Application

A. Using End Marks in Writing

Add periods, question marks, and exclamation points where necessary in the following paragraph. To add a period, insert this symbol ⊙. To add a question mark or an exclamation point, use a caret ^ and write the correct punctuation mark above it.

Have you ever seen or heard about an annual Vermont town meeting Every spring, around maple sugaring time, all the town's citizens meet in the town hall There they vote on any issue that concerns them, from rats in the town dump to school issues to international problems Even though a town has no responsibility for international relations, citizens express their opinions proudly What a way to practice democracy Oh, the town meeting is a grand social occasion, as well People get to meet and greet their neighbors after the long Vermont winter

CHAPTER 11

B. Using End Marks in an Outline

Imagine that you are considering running for public office. Write an outline to help yourself make up your mind. List three ways in which your running for office and serving in office will be good for your and your community. Also list three problems that might stop you from doing a good job in office. Be sure to punctuate correctly.

Title:

I Why I should run for office

A ______________

B ______________

C ______________

II Why I should not run for office

A ______________

B ______________

C ______________

Name ______________________ Date ______________

Commas in Sentences

Teaching

Use a comma before the conjunction that joins the two main clauses of a compound sentence. Do not use a comma to separate parts of a compound predicate.

Nurses used to be untrained, but now they must finish special training.

In a series of three or more items, use a comma after every item except the last one.

Nurses care for the sick, injured, and disabled.

Use commas between two or more adjectives of equal rank that modify the same noun. The adjectives are of equal rank if you can substitute the word *and* for the comma.

Nurses are well-trained, caring individuals.

Use commas after an introductory word or phrase.

After European nursing schools opened, Americans opened similar schools.

Use commas to set off one or more words that interrupt the flow of thought in a sentence.

Helping sick people, I believe, is a very worthy profession.

Use commas to set off nouns of direct address.

Robert, your mother and grandmother were both nurses.

Use commas to set off nonessential appositives. Appositives are nonessential if the meaning of the sentence is clear without them.

One group, the American Nurses' Association, admits only registered nurses.

Use a comma whenever the reader might otherwise be confused.

Before the mid–1900s, nursing was considered by many to be an unsuitable profession.

Using Commas Correctly

Insert commas where necessary in the following sentences.

1. During the Civil War in America Clara Barton aided in medical care for the Union.
2. She provided food medical supplies and nurses for the wounded soldiers.
3. She headed a government bureau the Missing Soldiers Office to find information on missing soldiers.
4. She even helped by the way to establish hospitals in Europe.
5. With Barton's help readers the American Red Cross Society was formed in 1881.
6. After studying nursing in London Edith Louisa Cavell became head of a training school in Brussels, Belgium.
7. When World War I began the school transformed itself into a Red Cross hospital.
8. Yes she treated wounded German and Allied soldiers alike.
9. The Germans took Brussels and they arrested her for housing Allied soldiers.
10. She was executed my friend despite international pleas for her life.

CHAPTER 11

Name ______________________ Date __________

Commas in Sentences

More Practice

A. Using Commas

Insert commas where necessary in the following sentences.

1. Elizabeth Kenny devised new more effective methods of treating infantile paralysis.
2. Kenny an Australian nurse aroused controversy due to her treatment methods.
3. Without any medical training she treated victims of polio in the bush country.
4. A pastor in Germany began an early nurses' training program Future Nurses.
5. Early nursing education however had little or no classroom preparation.
6. Training was based on apprenticeship and students learned from older students.
7. Nursing students provided hospitals with a needed low-cost service.
8. Hospital-based programs still exist but they do not grant an academic degree.
9. Nurses today work at hospitals schools camps homes and workplaces.
10. After completing an associate or baccalaureate degree program graduates can use the initials RN (registered nurse) after their name.

B. Using Commas in Writing

Rewrite the following paragraph, using commas where they are needed.

Florence Nightingale received her nursing training in Egypt and Germany. After the start of the Crimean War soldiers were dying because of inadequate medical care and rampant disease. She volunteered her services and the minister of war appointed her to head all nursing operations at the front. Her tireless heartfelt efforts saved many lives. Her contributions to nursing then and later were invaluable. Florence Nightingale was a nurse hospital reformer and humanitarian. Thanks to her I believe nursing became a respectable important profession.

____

____

____

____

____

____

____

Name ______________________________ Date ______________

Lesson 2

Commas in Sentences

Application

A. Writing with Complete Subjects and Complete Predicates

Add commas there they are needed in the following paragraph. Use the proofreading symbol ⁏ .

As members of one of the most populous professions in the nation registered nurses take on many duties. Student nurses can promote healthy living and they can aid patients recovering from illness or injury. After a physician sees a patient nurses carry out the orders for patient care. Nurses of course make independent decisions for patient care as well. Nurses can specialize in surgery pediatrics psychiatry or another specialty. The four types of advanced practice nurses are nurse practitioners certified nurse-midwives clinical nurse specialists and certified registered nurse anesthetists. These nurses advanced practice nurses can handle a wider range of services than registered nurses can. All nurses make essential, life-saving contributions to the practice of medicine.

B. Using Commas in Writing

Rewrite the sentences by following the directions in parentheses.

1. The nurse filled the supply closet. (Include a series of items.)

____

____

2. My family and I liked my grandfather's nurse. (Include two adjectives of equal rank that modify the same noun.)

____

3. The nurse practitioner was helpful. (Include another main clause.)

____

____

4. My nursing school was very competitive. (Include a nonessential appositive.)

____

____

CHAPTER 11

Name ______________________________ Date ______________

Lesson 3

Commas: Dates, Addresses, and Letters *Teaching*

Commas in Dates Use a comma between the day of the month and the year. If the sentence continues, use a comma after the year, also.

The play will be performed May 7, 2002, at the city auditorium.

Commas in Addresses Use a comma between the name of a city or town and the name of the state or country. If the sentence continues, use a comma after the name of the state or country.

Blaine, Pennsylvania, is home of the Blaine Wildcats.

Commas in Letters Use a comma after the greeting of a friendly letter and after the closing of a friendly or business letter.

Dear Uncle Fred, Your nephew,

A. Using Commas Correctly in Dates and Addresses

Insert commas where necessary in the following sentences.

1. The play is scheduled for December 19 2000 to January 9 2001 but there may be an extension.
2. The address of the auditorium is 75 Brinton Street Toledo Ohio.
3. The scene is set in a cowboy town—maybe Laredo Texas.
4. The playwright was born July 4 1960 in Brooklyn New York.
5. He said graduation was set for May 21 2001.
6. The only date I have memorized is the date I was born—August 4 1985.

B. Using Commas Correctly in Dates, Addresses, and Letters

Insert commas where necessary in the following letter.

2774 Melvin Avenue
Cleveland OH 44108
March 7 2000

Dear Sally

Thanks so much for inviting Grandpa Fritz and me to see your school play on May 7. Unfortunately we will be in San Francisco California that weekend for the convention Grandpa always likes to attend. But when you come to Cleveland—your mom said you'd come the weekend of June 12—I hope you'll tell us all about the play and recite your lines for us.

Fondly
Grandma Liz

CHAPTER 11

Name ______________________ Date __________

Lesson 3

Commas: Dates, Addresses, and Letters *More Practice*

A. Using Commas Correctly in Dates and Addresses

Insert commas where necessary in the following sentences.

1. Shakespeare's Globe Theater was on the south bank of the Thames in an area that is now a part of London England.
2. Shakespeare died on April 23 1616.
3. April 23 1564 is traditionally considered to have been his birthday.
4. The Little Theater Society of Dallas Texas honored his birthday with a program.
5. On May 12 2004 our local theater company will present a play by Jean Molière.
6. Molière's play *Tartuffe* was first performed on May 12 1664.
7. The work was presented at the royal palace of Versailles near Paris France.
8. Will any theater companies in New York New York observe the anniversary?

B. Using the Comma in Letters

Write these parts in the correct order on the lines below. Use commas where they are needed.

46 Leicester Avenue	Love	Thanks for your cards from Denver Colorado and San Francisco. It was a good thing you and Grandpa Fritz took your trip rather than come to see my play. Two days before opening night I got sick, and I was home in bed for a week. My stand-in got to play my part!
Sally	Dear Grandma Liz	
Toledo OH 43709	May 10 2000	

CHAPTER 11

Name ______________________________ Date ______________

Lesson 3

Commas: Dates, Addresses, and Letters

Application

A. Proofreading a Letter

Proofread the following letter for punctuation errors. Insert commas where necessary.

2774 Melvin Avenue
Cleveland OH 43724
May 13 2000

My dear Sally

Grandma Liz told me about your getting sick and losing your role in the school play. I don't know what I could say to console you except that I sympathize with how you feel. We know you would have been great. I found out on my 16th birthday that I wasn't an actor at all. On February 17 1950 I tried out for my school play. I didn't get any role. You did get a role and you will get another one next year! And we'll come see you, even if you're performing in Nome Alaska!

Love
Grandpa

CHAPTER 11

B. Writing with Commas

Imagine that you are William Shakespeare (1564–1616), and that you are having difficulty writing your first play. Write a letter to a friend back home in Stratford-upon-Avon, England, to talk about your current problem and your hopes for the future. On the lines below, write the letter. Use the form of a friendly letter, and use commas correctly.

____

____

____

____

____

____

____

____

____

____

____

____

Name ______________________ Date ____________

Punctuating Quotations

Teaching

A **direct quotation** is a report of a speaker's exact words. Use quotation marks at the beginning and at the end of a direct quotation.

> **"Movies about aliens are interesting," Jeff said.**

Use commas to set off the explanatory words used with a direct quotation, at the beginning, middle, or end of the quotation.

> **Jeff said, "Movies about aliens are interesting."**
>
> **"Movies about aliens," Jeff said, "are interesting."**

If the quotation itself is a question or exclamation, the question mark or exclamation point falls inside the end quotation marks. Commas and periods always go inside the end quotation marks.

> **"Wow!" Olivia exclaimed. "Did you read the new book about UFOs yet?"**

If the quotation is part of a question or exclamation, the question mark or exclamation point falls outside the end quotation marks.

> **Did the scientist say, "I believe aliens do exist"?**

A **divided quotation** is a direct quotation that is divided into two parts by explanatory words. Both parts are enclosed in quotation marks. The first word in the second part is not capitalized unless it begins a sentence. Review the above examples to see how to punctuate and capitalize a divided quotation.

A **dialogue** is a conversation between two or more speakers. In writing a dialogue, indicate a change in speaker by using a new paragraph and new set of quotation marks.

> **"Dr. Turner," the reporter asked, "do you believe in the existence of alien life?"**
>
> **"Yes, I believe it is possible intelligent life exists elsewhere," the scientist replied.**

An **indirect quotation** is a restatement, in somewhat different words, of what someone said. Do not use quotation marks to set off an indirect quotation.

> **Professor Reese announced that she didn't believe in UFOs or aliens.**

Using Quotation Marks

Add quotation marks where necessary in these sentences.

1. Alicia asked, Do you know what a UFO is?
2. A UFO, Isabella replied, is an alien spacecraft.
3. No! Ray cried. A UFO is any unidentified flying object.
4. Ninety percent of UFO sightings can later be identified, Ray added.
5. Did Ray say that 90 percent of UFO sightings can later be identified?
6. Some sightings, Sue said, are identified as birds, planes, satellites, or balloons.
7. How funny! Isabella exclaimed. Some of the sightings are just hoaxes, right?
8. You are right, Ray replied, but I think it would be exciting to see a real flying saucer.

CHAPTER 11

Name ______________________ Date ____________

Lesson 4

Punctuating Quotations

More Practice

A. Writing Sentences with Quotation Marks

Add quotation marks, commas, and end marks where necessary in each sentence. If the sentence is correct as is, circle the numeral before the sentence.

1. UFOs Elena stated have been sighted since ancient times.
2. Brian replied I can't believe people really think UFOs are alien spacecraft.
3. What! exclaimed Bernie. Did you know that the air force used to investigate UFOs as threats to our national security?
4. Elena and Brian admitted that they did not know about air force investigations.
5. Did they find anything Elena asked that they could not explain?
6. Out of 12,618 cases, the air force couldn't explain 701 sightings Bernie reports.
7. Did he just say The air force couldn't explain 701 sightings?
8. Bernie said That count was reported in 1969.
9. In 1997 Bernie announced the CIA admitted that the military had deceived people in an effort to keep high-altitude spying planes secret.
10. Wow! Brian exclaimed. I didn't realize that UFO sightings were so exciting.

CHAPTER 11

B. Using Quotation Marks

Copy this dialogue below, adding quotation marks where necessary.

A scientist has announced that her team will find intelligent life elsewhere in the universe.

Interesting! says Dr. Potts. I'd like to see how she plans to do this.

That claims Dr. Barbosa is preposterous. I don't believe she'll find anything.

Dr. Potts retorts Dr. Barbosa, the universe is large. Can't you admit that intelligent life might be out there somewhere?

No. I don't believe in any of these alien or UFO stories Dr. Barbosa replies.

I don't believe the stories either, but I do think aliens exist concludes Dr. Potts.

____

____

____

____

____

____

____

____

____

Name ______________________ Date ______

Punctuating Quotations

Application

A. Correcting Misuse of Quotation Marks

Rewrite the following sentences, using quotation marks, commas, and end marks correctly.

1. Darius said Books and movies about extraterrestrial life are fascinating and entertaining.

____

____

2. The great thing about alien stories added Gus is that almost anything can be possible.

____

____

3. Violet Mrs. Batista asked did you see the newspaper story about UFO sightings?

____

4. My favorite television shows are the ones that deal with aliens and outer space announced Owen.

____

____

5. Did Rosa say Let's rent the movie about the aliens hiding on Earth?

____

B. Writing with Quotation Marks

Write a short dialogue in which two students talk about how people are willing to believe in UFOs. Make sure that you indicate clearly who is speaking. Use quotation marks and other punctuation marks correctly.

____

____

____

____

____

____

____

CHAPTER 11

Name ______________________________ Date ______________

Lesson 5

Semicolons and Colons

Teaching

Semicolons in Compound Sentences Use a semicolon to join the parts of a compound sentence if you don't use a coordinating conjunction.

Fay cared for four cats; one of them actually belonged to a neighbor.

Use a semicolon between the parts of a compound sentence if the clauses are long and complicated, or if they contain one or more commas.

Fay had three cats of her own; but one of them, a gray one with black on his paws and ears, was her favorite.

Semicolons with Items in a Series When there are commas within parts of a series, use a semicolon to separate the parts.

In addition, she had a gerbil, a gift from her sister; a hamster, which she bought as a companion to the gerbil; and two white mice.

Colons Use a colon in the following ways: to introduce a list of items; after the formal greetings in a business letter, and between hours and minutes in expressions of time. When using the colon to introduce a list, use it only after nouns or pronouns.

Dear Mr. Jameson:

The lecture, which will begin at 11:30 A.M., is to cover three kinds of pets: felines, canines, and reptiles.

Using Semicolons and Colons

Add semicolons and colons where they are needed in the following sentences.

1. I don't mind cats, dogs, or fish but she wants to have lizards, snakes, and spiders.
2. We went to Paris we saw the Eiffel Tower.
3. Joan doesn't study she's unlikely to do well in math.
4. However, Joan is a good athlete she trains hard.
5. Before you set off for school, make sure you have all your supplies pencils, compass, protractor, notebooks.
6. Ask Mitzi to show you the tarantula she lets it walk up her arm.
7. The dogs get fed at 700 A.M. and 600 P.M.
8. Harvey walks Salt and Pepper, the dogs of our neighbor to the east and he feeds the fish in the aquarium of our neighbor to the west.
9. Your cats are companionable enough I still prefer a dog.
10. We went to two bookstores and a department store book section but the book I was looking for, about caring for and training dogs, wasn't anywhere.
11. My father is from Atlanta, Georgia my mother is from Portland, Maine and I was born in Chicago.
12. Memorize the following your locker location, its number, and the lock combination.

Name ______________________________ Date ______________

Lesson 5

Semicolons and Colons

More Practice

A. Using the Semicolon and the Colon

Add semicolons and colons where they are needed in the numbered sentences.

(1) Keeping a pet is a big responsibility it's a commitment for the life of the animal. **(2)** Caring for the pet demands more than just putting out food and water those are just the basics. **(3)** You also have to think about such things as the following vaccinations, the babysitting of your pet when you're away, and veterinary care.

(4) These items can cost a good deal of money in addition, you should also consider the emotional cost, to you and the rest of the family, of a crisis involving a pet. **(5)** A cat or dog may get hit by a car, especially in the city, where there are more vehicles or your pet may be injured in a fight with another animal, either in the country or the city. If you remember these drawbacks and still want a pet, there are hundreds of animal shelters and pet stores to serve you.

B. Using the Semicolon and the Colon in Writing

On the line at the right, write the word(s) from the sentence that should be followed by a semicolon or colon. Write the correct punctuation mark following each word. If the sentence is punctuated correctly, write **Correct.**

EXAMPLE This store sells toys for pets catnip for cats, rubber bones for dogs, and tiny bells for birds. *pets:*

1. Before buying Izzy, we bought a book on training dogs the book has already been extremely helpful ______________
2. The book covers all the basics nutrition, medical care, and what to do in case of an accident or injury. ______________
3. It came with a gift certificate for a really useful item that is, a dozen cans of dog food and a list of other free pet items. ______________
4. We didn't have reserved seats for the dog show consequently, we couldn't get in. ______________
5. According to the newspaper report of the show, we could have seen all these dogs poodles, Pomeranians, bulldogs, Yorkshire terriers, and salukis. ______________

CHAPTER 11

Name ______________________ Date __________

Semicolons and Colons

Application

A. Proofreading a Play Review

The following is a review of a fable play, a play in which the characters are animals. However, the critic who wrote the review used an old-fashioned typewriter on which the key holding the colon and semicolon didn't work. Copyedit his review, adding the needed semicolons and colons. Then rewrite the article correctly.

In this play, Reynard the fox is clever, as usual the chicken is a bit more intelligent than usual. The play includes several other traditional fable characters a duck, a cow, and even a frog. The central focus is on the contest of wits between the fox and the chicken and the chicken, with a little help from the other animals, wins out in the end. The costumes are clever however, the staging is dull. But it's a cute play and children and adults, too, if they have any sense of fun, will enjoy it.

____

____

____

____

____

____

B. Writing Sentences with Semicolons and Colons

On a separate sheet of paper, write a sentence for each item, matching the description in parentheses.

Example (sentence that uses a semicolon to join the parts of a compound sentence without a coordinating conjunction)
The play will be held in the gym; the stage crew has set up folding chairs on the basketball court.

1. (sentence that uses a colon in an expression of time)
2. (sentence that uses a semicolon to separate parts when commas appear within parts of a series)
3. (sentence that uses a semicolon to join the parts of a compound sentence without a coordinating conjunction)
4. (sentence that uses a colon to introduce a list of items)

Name ______________________ Date ______________

Hyphens, Dashes, and Parentheses

Teaching

Here are ways to use the hyphen, the dash, and parentheses.

Hyphens Use a hyphen if part of a word must be carried over from one line to the next. Only words of two syllables or more may be broken, and each syllable must have at least two letters. Make sure that the word is separated between syllables.

Correct: cur- rent styl- ish be- fore
Incorrect: curr- ent sty- le a- gain

Use hyphens in certain compound words, such as *self-starter* and *make-believe.*
Use hyphens in compound numbers from twenty-one through ninety-nine.
Use hyphens in spelled-out fractions, such as *one-fifth* and *two-sevenths.*

Dashes Use dashes to show an abrupt break in thought.

This dress—my goodness—is made of silk.

Parentheses Use parentheses to set off material that is loosely related to the rest of the sentence.

Saddle shoes (which are white with a black stripe) were popular in the 1950s.

A. Using the Hyphen in Compound Words and Fractions

Write each of these words and phrases correctly, adding hyphens where needed.

1. thirty four dollars ______________________
2. one quarter of an inch ______________________
3. my great grandmother's wedding dress ______________________
4. a run down pair of shoes ______________________

B. Using the Hyphen in Words Broken Between Lines

Underline each word that is broken correctly for use at the end of a line.

1. cott-on, flap-per, san-dal, fash-ion, le-ather
2. ray-on, si-lk, ove-ralls, ny-lon, cost-ume, den-im

C. Using the Dash and Parentheses

Add dashes or parentheses where they are needed in these sentences.

1. This sweater a rather expensive item is made of angora.
2. My prom dress whether you believe it or not was once very fashionable.
3. My favorite clothing fad you may like it too is bobby socks and poodle skirts.
4. Bell-bottoms pants with wide bottoms were quite popular in the 1970s.
5. That hat if we can ever find it in this attic is the one that I wore nearly every day as a young girl.

CHAPTER 11

Name ______________________________ Date ______________

Lesson 6

Hyphens, Dashes, and Parentheses *More Practice*

A. Using the Hyphen in Compound Words and Fractions

Write each of these words and phrases correctly, adding hyphens where needed.

1. seventy six yards ______________________________

2. denim bell bottoms ______________________________

3. three quarter length ______________________________

4. forty seven percent cotton ______________________________

5. fast forward to possible future trends ______________________________

B. Using the Dash and Parentheses

Add dashes and parentheses where they are needed in these sentences.

1. When you were younger you might remember this you always wore your hat backwards.

2. The burnoose which is a loose, hooded robe is very practical in the Middle East.

3. The gown you will notice if you look closely is covered with blue sequins.

4. The shirts these are all cotton should be washed in the delicate cycle.

5. Leisure suits do you know what they looked like? were popular in the 1970s.

C. Using the Hyphen, Dash, and Parentheses Correctly

Rewrite each sentence, correcting punctuation errors. If a word at the end of a line is broken incorrectly, but there is a correct way of breaking it, show the word broken correctly in your revision. If the word may not be broken, move it to the second line.

1. Silk which originally came from Chin- ______________________________

a) is a rather expensive and delic- ______________________________

ate material. ______________________________

2. When a silkworm—it is a variety of ______________________________

moth caterpillar makes its coc- ______________________________

oon, it forms silk fibers. ______________________________

3. Wool is a material made from she- ______________________________

ep's hair. ______________________________

4. Wool it is a quite warm material ______________________________

is a very common textile for ma- ______________________________

king, winter sweaters. ______________________________

CHAPTER 11

Name ______________________________ Date ______________

Hyphens, Dashes, and Parentheses

Application

A. Proofreading for Correct Punctuation

Rewrite this paragraph on the lines below, adding or correcting the placement of hyphens, dashes, and parentheses as needed.

Some fashion designers you may be able to think of some design clothes that are casual, yet elegant. Many designers have perfumes do you wear perfume? as well as clothes. My favorite designer is a leader of *haute couture* (high fashion. One famous designer got his start designing ties. It usually takes years to get a famous name if a designer is lucky, his or her name may become famous within a few years of entering the fashion business.

____

____

____

____

____

____

B. Writing with Correct Punctuation

Follow the directions to write and punctuate sentences correctly.

1. Write a sentence that requires a hyphen.

____

____

2. Write a sentence that requires dashes and at least one hyphen.

____

____

3. Write a sentence that requires a hyphen and parentheses.

____

____

4. Write a sentence that requires a hyphen and dashes.

____

____

CHAPTER 11

Name ______________________________ Date ______________

Lesson 7

Apostrophes

Teaching

Apostrophes in Possessives Use an apostrophe to form the possessive of any noun, whether singular or plural. For a singular noun, add *'s* even if the word ends in *s*.

the director**'s** script   Thomas**'s** entrance

For plural nouns that end in *s*, add only an apostrophe.

the actors**'** needs   the ushers**'** names

For plural nouns that do not end in *s*, add an apostrophe and *s*.

the women**'s** notebooks   the crowd**'s** cheers

Apostrophes in Contractions Use an apostrophe in a contraction to show where a letter or letters have been left out.

I will→I'll   we have→we've   they are→they're   he is→he's

Don't confuse contractions with possessive nouns, which do not contain apostrophes.

it's (contraction, means *it is*)   its (possessive, means *belonging to it*)

Apostrophes in Plurals Use an apostrophe plus *s* to form the plurals of letters and words referred to as words.

In that fancy writing, the *f*'s look like *s*'s.
We had to reprint the poster because it had two *the's* in a row.

CHAPTER 11

Using Apostrophes

In each sentence below, underline the word that correctly completes the sentence.

1. This is (Tess' / Tess's) opening night.
2. (It's / Its) her first lead role.
3. I know (shell / she'll) do fine.
4. Please find out (whose / who's) tickets these are.
5. (Your / You're) going to enjoy this play.
6. How many (*e*'s / *e*s) are there in Tennessee?
7. The (subscribers / subscribers') tickets are in the red box.
8. You know (their / they're) going to expect special treatment.
9. The production staff has (its / it's) work to do.
10. Did you remember the different (actors' / actor's) costume sizes?
11. The program tells (whose / who's) playing each part.
12. I (can't / cant) remember a funnier play.
13. The (men's / mens') chorus didn't get the right music.
14. We ran out of letters for the marquee; we had to use (*1*'s / *1*s) for (*l*s / *l*'s).
15. Jo asked if (were / we're) going out afterwards.

Name ______________________________ Date ____________

Lesson 7

Apostrophes

More Practice

A. Using Apostrophes Correctly

In each sentence below, underline the word that uses an apostrophe incorrectly or should have an apostrophe but does not. Then write the word correctly on the line.

1. The crew wanted to express it's thanks to the director. ____________

2. The actors for once remembered they're lines. ____________

3. The ladies costumes were hilarious. ____________

4. Joyce' part was hard to play. ____________

5. We found Carlos book bag. ____________

6. Whose in charge here, anyway? ____________

7. Its a play that can't miss. ____________

8. We all know who's script it was. ____________

9. Is this the childrens bus? ____________

10. Their going to be tired and hungry. ____________

B. Using Apostrophes in Possessives

Rewrite this paragraph on the lines below, replacing all underlined phrases with phrases using possessives with apostrophes.

Going to the theater is a hobby of my friend Maria. She likes to attend the first night of a play. Then she compares her review with the review of the newspaper critic. The goal of Maria is to see one play per week. She never misses productions of comedies and tragedies of Shakespeare. She volunteers to usher at two theaters. Sometimes the schedules of the two theaters conflict. Then Maria has to choose between two plays. Making a choice like that is a nightmare of a theater-lover.

Name ______________________ Date ____________

Lesson 7

Apostrophes

Application

A. Proofreading for Use of the Apostrophe

Proofread the paragraph below for errors in the use of apostrophes. If a word uses an apostrophe incorrectly or is lacking a needed apostrophe, cross out the word. Then draw a caret ^ next to the error and write the word correctly above the error.

The senior highs drama students decided theyd put on Eugene O'Neills *Ah, Wilderness!* this year. Its his only comedy and some critic's favorite. Theatergoer's enjoy the story of a young man—he plays hero—on the brink of falling in love, and his parents reaction to this rather disturbing event in they're lives. The students choice was a good one. Everyone whose seen the play has liked it. In fact, Im planning to go back next Saturday to see one of the last performances'. They're is a matinee and an evening performance Saturday.

B. Using Apostrophes in Writing

First rewrite each phrase listed below, using a possessive with an apostrophe. Then use the phrases that you created in a paragraph about a mishap in a restaurant.

the specialty of the chef ______________________

the food of the customer ______________________

the tray of the waiter ______________________

the foot of a long-legged man ______________________

the apologies of the waiter ______________________

____

____

____

____

____

____

____

____

____

CHAPTER 11

Name ______________________ Date __________

Lesson 8

Punctuating Titles

Teaching

Quotation marks, italics, and underlining used correctly in titles show what kind of work or selection is named.

Quotation Marks Use quotation marks to set off the titles of short works.

Book chapter	"The Sailboat Race," from *Stuart Little*	**Magazine article**	"Travel the Unbeaten Path"
Short story	"Dr. Jekyll and Mr. Hyde"	**Song**	"Star Spangled Banner"
Essay	"Civil Disobedience"	**Poem**	"O Captain! My Captain"

Italics and Underlining Use italics for titles of longer works and for the names of ships, trains, spacecraft, and individual airplanes (not the type of plane). In handwriting, use underlining to indicate words that should be in italics in printed material.

Book	*A Tale of Two Cities*	**Epic poem**	*The Iliad*
Play	*My Fair Lady*	**Painting**	*View of Toledo*
Magazine	*Newsweek*	**Ship**	*Lusitania*
Movie	*Beauty and the Beast*	**Train**	*Super Chief*
Long musical selection or CD	*Victory at Sea*	**Airplane or Spacecraft**	*Endeavour*

CHAPTER 11

Punctuating Titles Correctly

Write each sentence, using quotation marks or underlining correctly to set off titles.

1. Did Mr. Talbot see Death of a Salesman when it was on Broadway?

____

2. Thoreau wrote Civil Disobedience and the much longer work, Walden.

____

3. The guest star sang People Will Say We're in Love from the musical Oklahoma!

____

4. View of Toledo is by the great Spanish painter El Greco.

____

5. O Captain! My Captain! is a poem by Walt Whitman.

____

6. We rode the Orient Express to Istanbul.

____

7. Mark Twain wrote the historical novel The Prince and the Pauper.

____

Name ______________________ Date ____________

Lesson 8

Punctuating Titles

More Practice

A. Punctuating Titles Correctly

In each sentence below, insert quotation marks where needed and underline words that should be italicized.

1. How many times has Abby read Little Women?
2. Do you know why The Surprise Symphony got that name?
3. Clare loves the poem Eletelephony.
4. NASA built the Endeavour following the explosion of the Challenger.
5. The Gift of the Magi is a famous short story by O. Henry.
6. Have you ever seen Pablo Picasso's famous antiwar painting Guernica?
7. Naomi read Robert Frost's poem Stopping by Woods on a Snowy Evening.
8. George Gershwin wrote music not only for Broadway musicals such as Of Thee I Sing, but also for the concert hall, for example, Rhapsody in Blue.
9. When exactly did the Titanic sink?
10. There is a famous song called City of New Orleans.

CHAPTER 11

B. Punctuating Titles Correctly

Use each title given in parentheses in a sentence, punctuating the title correctly.

1. (traditional song: Yankee Doodle) ______________________

____

2. (book by L. Frank Baum: The Wizard of Oz) ______________________

____

3. (short story by Washington Irving: The Legend of Sleepy Hollow) ______________________

____

4. (poem by Edgar Allan Poe: The Raven) ______________________

____

5. (cruise ship: Queen Mary) ______________________

____

6. (play by William Shakespeare: A Midsummer Night's Dream) ______________________

____

Name ______________________________ Date ______________

Lesson 8

Punctuating Titles

Application

A. Punctuating Titles Correctly

Even good friends may have different tastes in books, music, movies, and so on. In the chart below, write your own favorites in the various categories listed. Then write the name of a friend or family member and list his or her favorites, too. (Be sure to ask the person about his or her choices first.) Use quotation marks or underlining to show italics.

	My Favorite	___________'s Favorite
Book		
Short Story		
Ship		
Movie		
Song		
CD or Tape		
Poem		
Play		

B. Punctuating Titles Correctly in Writing

Review the chart above. Then write a paragraph in which you identify which of the choices were easy and which were difficult. Mention some of the other works that you wanted to include in the chart. Or, if you have enough information from the friend or family member referred to in the chart, write the paragraph discussing his or her choices.

CHAPTER 11

Name ______________________ Date ______________

Sentence Parts

More Practice 1

Complete each diagram with the sentence provided.

A. Simple Subjects and Verbs

Artists paint.

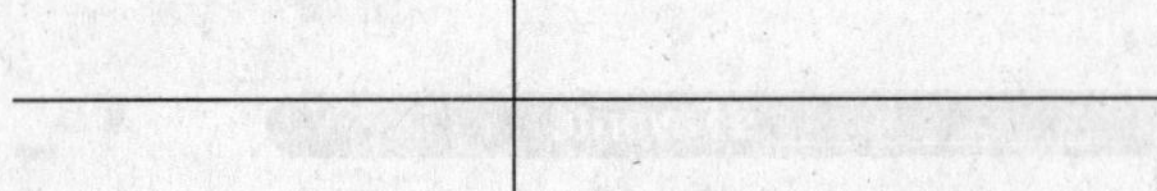

B. Compound Subjects and Verbs

Compound Subject Teachers and students paint.

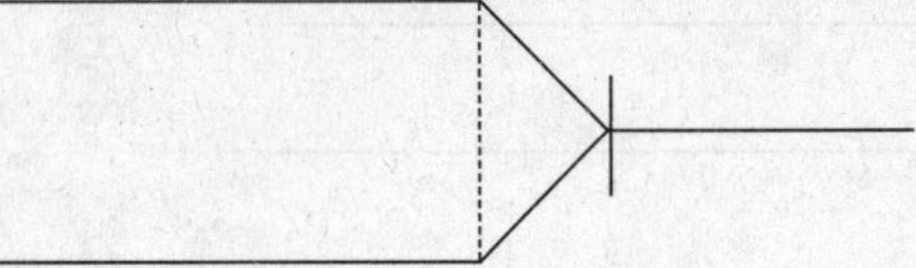

Compound Verb Artists sketch and paint.

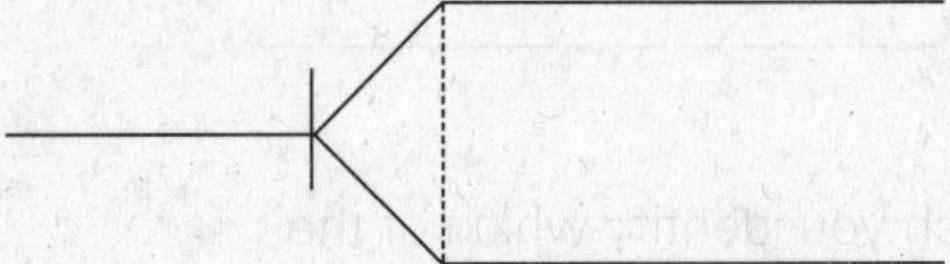

Compound Subject and Verb Teachers and students sketch and paint.

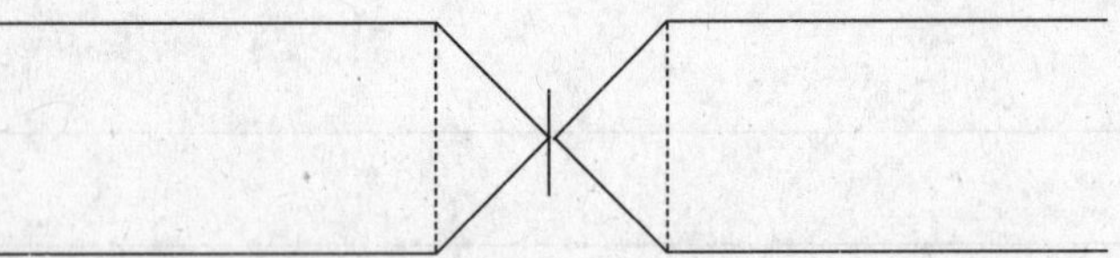

C. Adjectives and Adverbs

Many art students work hard here.

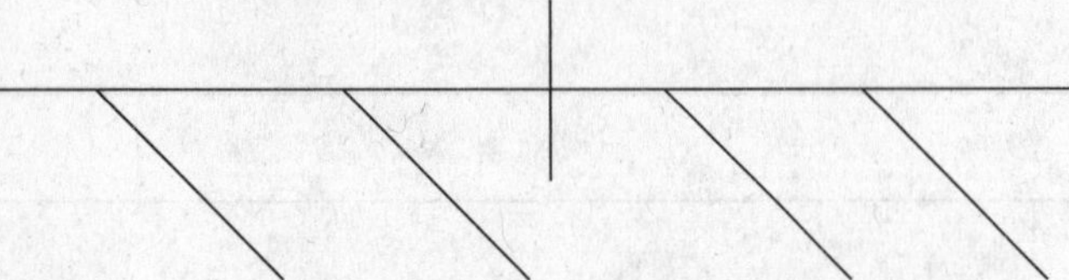

CHAPTER 11

Name ______________________ Date __________

Sentence Parts

More Practice 2

Complete each diagram with the sentence provided.

D. Subject Complements

Predicate Noun Claude Monet was a painter.

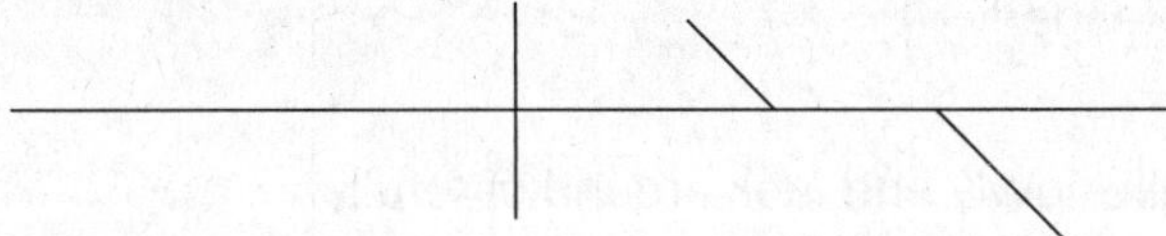

Predicate Adjective Monet became famous.

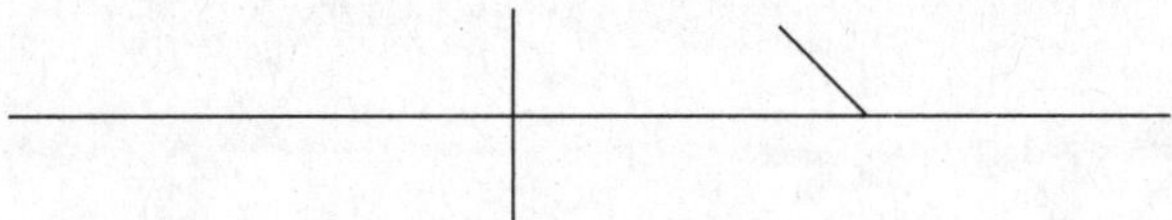

E. Direct Objects

Single Direct Object Monet skillfully painted beautiful waterlilies.

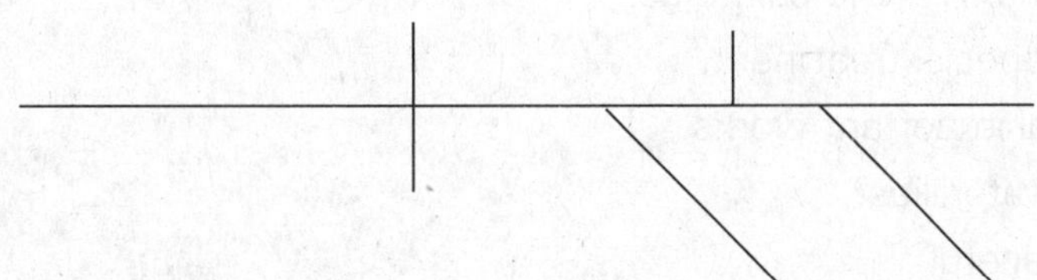

Compound Direct Object Museum-goers enjoy Monet's paintings and other works.

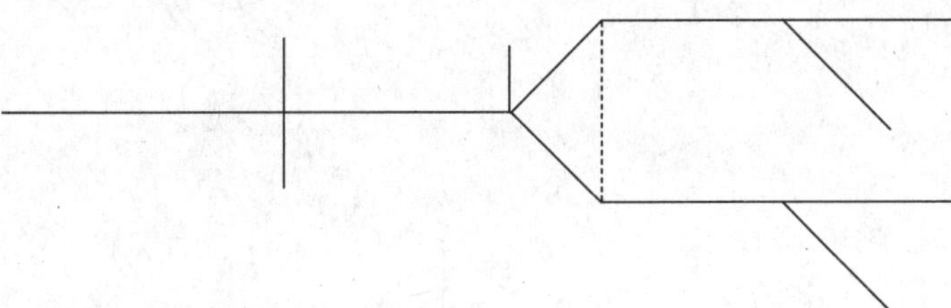

F. Indirect Objects

Art museums have provided visitors many pleasant hours.

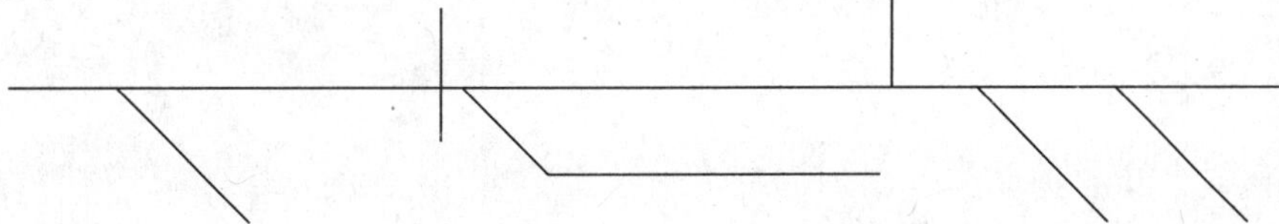

CHAPTER 11

Name ______________________________ Date ______________

Sentence Parts *Application*

On a separate piece of paper, diagram each of these sentences.

A. Diagramming Subjects, Verbs, and Modifiers

1. A special show opens today.
2. Museum members and other visitors arrive eagerly.
3. All visitors enter here and turn right.
4. Young museum-goers and older visitors walk slowly and look around carefully.

B. Diagramming Subject Complements and Objects

1. This large room is their goal.
2. These paintings are very valuable.
3. The paintings give museum-goers pleasure.
4. This special exhibit includes paintings and their preliminary sketches.

C. Mixed Practice

1. Art museums also exhibit statues and other works.
2. Dry air and bright lights may harm some paintings.
3. Museums give these works special treatment.
4. That guide showed us several important works.
5. My favorites were Monet's waterlilies.
6. An Indian statue was very graceful.
7. The museum shop sells visitors attractive posters and other souvenirs.
8. When will you visit the art museum?

Name ____________________ Date ____________

Phrases and Clauses

More Practice 1

Complete each diagram with the sentence provided.

A. Prepositional Phrases

Adjective Prepositional Phrases Certain buildings of unusual beauty are famous worldwide.

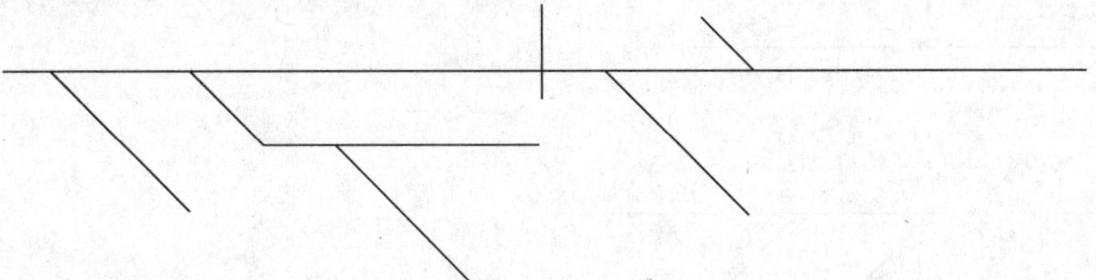

Adverb Prepositional Phrases Spectacular ancient temples have been found in Cambodia.

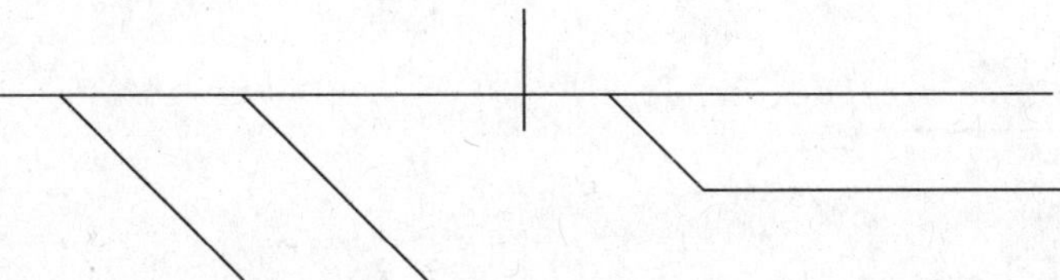

CHAPTER 11

B. Compound Sentences

The temples of Angkor were built before 1200, and since 1860 many of them have been restored to their original beauty.

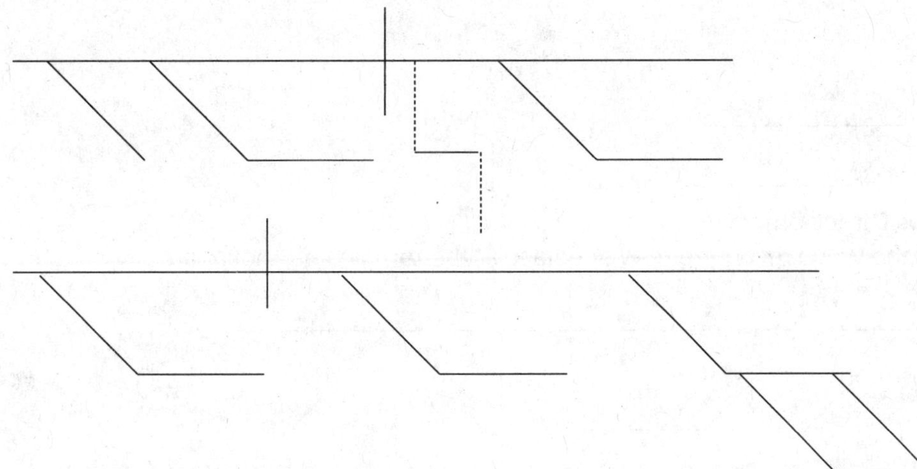

Name ______________________ Date ____________

Phrases and Clauses

More Practice 2

Complete each diagram with the sentence provided.

C. Complex Sentences

Adjective Clause Angkor Wat, which is the largest temple in ancient Angkor, has a pyramid form.

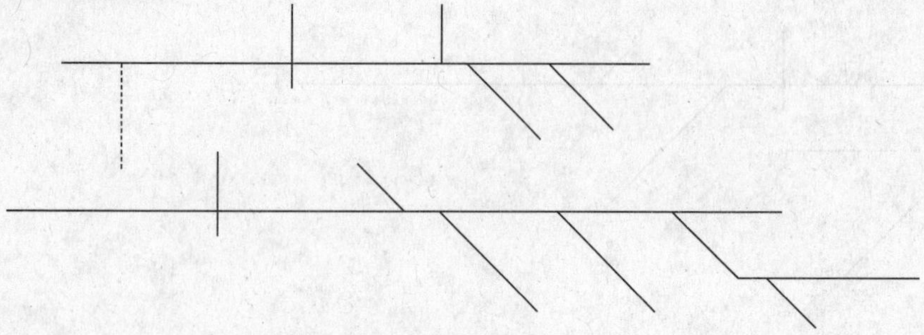

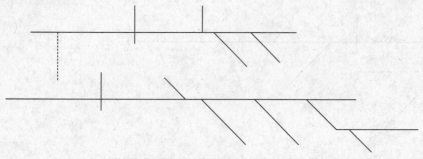

Adverb Clause Angkor was abandoned after its people were defeated in war.

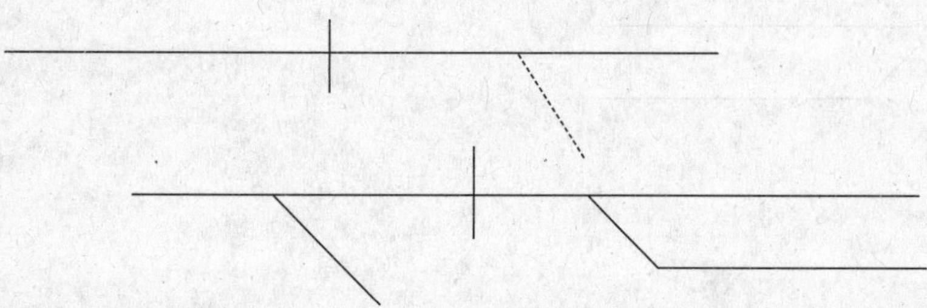

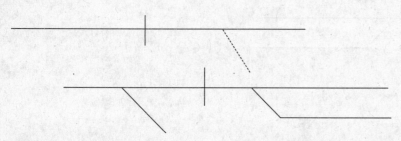

Noun Clause Used as Subject Where the city stood was forgotten for centuries.

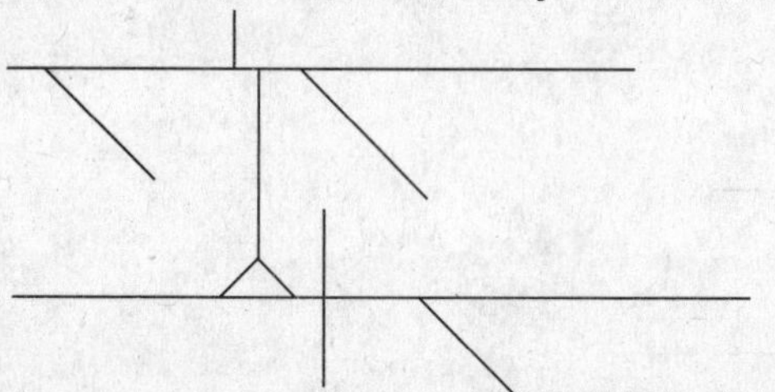

Noun Clause Used as Direct Object
Today people around the world recognize how spectacular the temples of Angkor are.

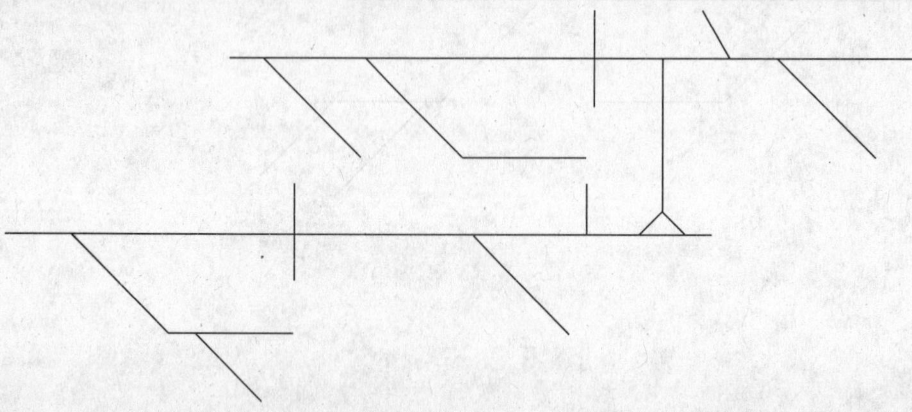

CHAPTER 11

Name ______________________ Date ____________

Phrases and Clauses

Application

On a separate piece of paper, diagram each of these sentences.

A. Diagramming Prepositional Phrases and Compound Sentences

1. The ancient Greeks built many beautiful buildings, and one of them is the Parthenon.
2. This marble structure was completed in Athens, Greece, around 440 B.C.
3. The Parthenon first was used as a temple, and later the building became a church.
4. Today, unfortunately, the Parthenon is in ruins.

B. Diagramming Complex Sentences

1. The Parthenon was dedicated to Athena, who was the protector of Athens.
2. This goddess symbolized whatever was wise and beautiful.
3. The building still stands on a hill that overlooks Athens.
4. How the Parthenon was badly damaged is a sad story.

C. Mixed Practice

1. After most Greeks became Christians, the Parthenon was used as a church.
2. Then Turkish Muslims captured Athens, and the building became a mosque.
3. In 1687, Italian forces attacked Athens.
4. Gunpowder that was stored in the Parthenon blew up.
5. Most of the building was destroyed, but its outside columns survived.
6. When the Parthenon was built, its walls were covered with sculptures.
7. After the explosion, many of the sculptures were moved to the British Museum in London.
8. Whoever visits the ruins of the Parthenon now is still impressed by its beauty.